Twayne's Theatrical Arts Series

Warren French
EDITOR

Ken Russell

Ken Russell directing *The Music Lovers* (1970)

Ken Russell

GENE D. PHILLIPS

Loyola University of Chicago

BOSTON

Twayne Publishers

1979

Ken Russell

is first published in 1979 by Twayne Publishers,
A Division of G. K. Hall & Co.

Copyright © 1979 by G. K. Hall & Co.

Printed on permanent / durable acid-free paper and bound
in the United States of America

First Printing, October 1979

Library of Congress Cataloging in Publication Data

Phillips, Gene D
Ken Russell.
(Twayne's theatrical arts series)
Bibliography: p. 185-89
Includes index.
1. Russell, Ken, 1927-
PN1998.A3R776   791.43′0233′0924   79-4626
ISBN 0-8057-9266-X

Contents

About the Author

GENE D. PHILLIPS first met Ken Russell while the director was supervising the editing of *The Music Lovers* in London in the spring of 1970. After that first interview, one of the first extensive interviews with Russell to appear in the United States, the author met and interviewed the director several more times over the succeeding years, and watched the shooting of *The Boy Friend*. In addition Russell has kept up a correspondence with the author during this same period in which he has detailed interesting experiences that have surrounded the making of each of his subsequent films as well as discussed projects which ultimately were not realized.

The author is an elected member of the Society for Cinema Studies and teaches fiction and film at Loyola University of Chicago. He received his doctorate in English from Fordham University in New York City and has been chosen to serve on juries at the Cannes, Berlin, and Chicago Film Festivals. He has published more than fifty articles on literature and the film and is a contributing editor of *Literature / Film Quarterly*.

His books include *The Movie Makers: Artists in an Industry* and *Evelyn Waugh's Officers, Gentlemen, and Rogues: The Fact behind His Fiction* (both published by Nelson-Hall of Chicago); *Graham Greene: The Films of His Fiction* (Columbia University Teachers College Press); *Stanley Kubrick: A Film Odyssey* in an original and also an expanded edition (both published by Popular Library of New York); and *Tennessee Williams and the Movies* (Fairleigh Dickinson University Press of New Jersey and Tantivy Press of London).

His contributions to books include the essay on homosexuality in *Sexuality and the Movies* (Indiana University Press); and essays in *Ingmar Bergman: Essays in Criticism* (Oxford University Press of New York) and *Science Fiction Films* (Simon and Schuster of New York).

Editor's Foreword

THIS BOOK might most appropriately borrow the title of Robert Philip Kohler's essay "Ken Russell's Biopics" (*Film Comment*, 1973), for, as Gene Phillips stresses, Russell's principal achievement from his earliest telefilms for the BBC has been sharing with the world his extraordinary personal visions of a procession of the world's most colorful and controversial artists. Indeed, with the exception of *The Boy Friend*, all of Russell's memorable work for television and the cinema has been "biopics," for even *Tommy* is the life story of a new culture hero that has developed since the great stars of rock music have attained mythical status since World War II.

Since there is almost nothing to be said about this primary aspect of Russell's work that is not said better in the book that follows, frequently by Russell himself in excerpts from his long correspondence with the author that share with us much about his artistic intentions, I may perhaps be excused on this occasion for using this foreword to precede the main event with a kind of mini-book testimonial to the power of Ken Russell's creations. Were there "world enough and time," Russell is one of the filmmakers that I would have particularly liked to write about myself, as I have already written briefly about *The Boy Friend* as a "nonlinear film" in *Arts in Society* (Summer-Fall 1973). One of the wisest and most rewarding decisions that I have been able to make in developing this series, however, has been to turn this project over to Gene Phillips, whose long friendship and shared concerns with Ken Russell has made possible this unusually close-up look at a controversial and often puzzling artist at work.

My book would take a much different tack; for I am a poor biographer. Uncomfortable too close to others, I prefer to explore the transactions that can occur between the viewer and the work of art. Were I writing about my experiences with Russell's films, I would want to call the book *The Magic of Ken Russell*, because the reason that for me Russell is the director who will always be most strongly associated with the early 1970s, as Fellini is with the 1960s and Robert Altman, with the years since *Nashville*, is that I have always prized above the other capacities of film its magical ability that George Méliès discovered can take us into a world that exists nowhere else. I take quite seriously the notion that Jean-Luc Godard has bandied about that, contrary to conventional views, the Lumière Brothers are the fathers of the "fiction" film, while Méliès is the father of the realistic documentary, because no film can ever capture all of reality external to it, so that "documentaries" must be fantasies shaped to accord with the filmmakers' particular perceptions of the world, while films like *Juliet of the Spirits*, *The Devils*, *Buffalo Bill and the Indians*, and Louis Malle's *Black Moon* can—in gifted hands—document a reality that is complete because it has no other dimension and would otherwise be trapped in the heads of its creators. I welcome with joy those inheritors of the Méliès tradition because they surpass our private dreams in their projections of dreams that can be shared.

Nowhere is Ken Russell's extraordinary gift as a visionary artist better revealed than in his explanation to Gene Phillips about his conception of *The Devils*: "I don't mind now if I am able to make the film or not since I have worked it out shot by shot in my imagination. *I can run it in my head any time I want to*" (italics mine). Even if, as Russell goes on to acknowledge, "a finished film is often very different from the way one has initially pictured it in one's mind," the project springs from a conception that exists in the mind of its creator *in the form of a moving picture* and not as a cluster of verbal ideas to be "illustrated" with pictures. The making of the film constitutes a liberating of this vision which could not be shared in any other form. (Alfred Hitchcock has also spoken of his thus envisioning his films in advance of their production.)

Ken Russell took me by the surprise that he took most Americans who had not had any chance to see his early "biopics" for the BBC. (By one of those staggering coincidences that keep life ever suspenseful, however, the very day that I received Gene Phillips's manuscript, I had my first opportunity to see one of Russell's telefilms, "Isadora Duncan: The Biggest Dancer in the World," on the New Hampshire Public Broadcasting station, affording me a rare chance to compare an original with a critical account when both were entirely new to me.)

I became excited about Russell, however, even later than others. I passed up *Billion Dollar Brain*, his first film generally circulated in the United States; but did go in April 1970 to see *Women in Love*, curious to see what might have happened to the D. H. Lawrence novel after the strange things that had happened to his *Sons and Lovers*. Although this first big commercial success of Russell's career is one of his most critically esteemed pictures also, I was not particularly taken with it. It struck me as too Lawrencian, not really very adventuresome cinematically (despite the boldness of the nude wrestling scene). It was a year, however, of perhaps the greatest political unrest that this country has experienced in my lifetime (the Kent State killings were to occur the next month); and *Women in Love* seemed to me too remote and pastoral to compete with Luchino Visconti's *The Damned* and Costa-Gavras's Z that I had seen just previously. It did not even make me conscious of Ken Russell as a force to be reckoned with. Later visitors brought tantalizing rumors about *The Music Lovers*, but the film failed to penetrate our Midwestern redoubt.

I was utterly unprepared, therefore, when, a year and a half later, I was attracted by others' scandalized reactions to a film passing through town, *The Devils*, that I knew I would have to see in a hurry if it disappeared as quickly as most attractions that appeal to mature audiences. I was absolutely stunned by what I saw. I could not believe that this was happening on the screen, and I became entirely converted to the mythmaking powers of Ken Russell. And soon I learned, too, having returned from Russell's dream of Loudon to the nightmare puerilities of Indianapolis, that there was cause to fight as well the incomprehensible reactions of those who took the film literally. How could those hygienically white walls be seen except as the symbolic embodiment of the magic barrier that we pray will isolate us from the machinations of the world's devils? What Russell had achieved here was something virtually unparalleled on the screen—something that had eluded even such literary masters as William Faulkner and John Steinbeck in novels—the fleshing-out of an allegory with a story that did indeed make our flesh creep at the same time that it gave us something worth thinking about.

Then at regular six-month intervals in April and November, there appeared, as harbingers of spring, the musicals *The Boy Friend* and *Tommy* and, as a portent of winter, the stony *Savage Messiah*. I have finally no alternative but to believe that I like *The Boy Friend* better than anyone else in the world (better even than its maker, from Gene Phillips's account in this book). With its dazzling tributes to British theatrical and American cinematic traditions, it seems to me an absolutely flawless capturing of the motivating spirit behind the improbably spectacle of the singing theater.

Savage Messiah, on the other hand, which Gene Phillips and many others rank high among Russell's works, is to my flamboyant tastes too much of a letdown after the expectations aroused by *The Devils* and *The Boy Friend* and fulfilled once more by *Tommy* and *The Music Lovers*, which I finally caught up with in a most appropriate setting at New York's Carnegie Hall Cinema. I was awed by the evidence *Savage Messiah* offers (as I see in retrospect *Women in Love* does also) of Russell's extraordinary ability to change his style and pace—the broadness of a vision that will not be stereotyped. Perhaps Russell's pacing is the most remarkable of his gifts. As Gene Phillips points out there are serene moments even in *The Devils*, but one forgets them out of their context as one effaces also the worst of the horrors; what remains, years later, is the sense of irresistible movement. Russell never puts on the brakes (*Tommy* becomes almost unbearable); his films never drag or falter. They move with the speed of dreams over a landscape into which few dreamers have dared to venture.

Owing to the vagaries of American distribution, I have never been able to see *Mahler* or *Lisztomania*. As for *Valentino*, I can say only that it is a marvel. Regrettably, it is a generally unappreciated marvel, though I hope that the account Gene Phillips gives of it here as the climactic achievement of Ken Russell's heroic search so far will win new attention and respect for the unflagging inventiveness that combines gaudy, often vulgar spectacle with an account of personal integrity so serious that it would have turned leaden in most well-intentioned hands to give substance to the legend of the 1920s through one of its most glamorous and tragic figures. Russell gives us, of course, not the Twenties as they were, but as they live in dreams. The evocation that haunts me most is neither the famous jail sequence nor the boxing bout, both of which Gene Phillips properly singles out for attention, but that dimly opalescent view of thousands of frustrated women howling across the hills beneath Valentino's bedroom window on his second wedding night. It never happened, but it is more true than anything that did.

Thus "Ken Russell and I," which I fear contains—like many testimonials—much more of me than of the magic-maker. Let me turn you over now to Gene Phillips, who can, with modest affection, tell you much more about Ken Russell and his creations, subjects as well worth getting acquainted with as those that Russell has celebrated in his biopics.

W. F.

Preface

IT HAS OFTEN been said that if all of the films of a good director were laid end to end, the result would not be a group of separate films but a series of installments in the same film. This is just another way of saying that it is the director, more than anyone else involved in the production of a film, who leaves his personal stamp on a motion picture. For it is the director, after all, who must create a unified work of art from all of the varied contributions of actors and technicians.

Andrew Sarris, one of the most articulate champions of the film director's vital role in the filmmaking process, has said that "only the director can provide a unity of style out of all the diverse ingredients at his disposal. The script writer will find his words chopped up into shots. The actor who performs continuously on the stage is recorded intermittently on the set, where his part is slowly eroded out of sequence into little bits and pieces."

Consequently, it is the director alone who can and must confer artistic unity on a motion picture. A director who uses cinematic techniques in this fashion to express his personal vision of reality in film after film, moreover, in time builds up a coherent body of work like that which a novelist produces. This is certainly true of Ken Russell; and hence one's appreciation of a given Russell film can be greatly enhanced when it is examined in the context of his total body of work, as the ensuing pages attempt to show.

"The fact that most directors do not write their own scripts is enough to discredit the role of the director in the eyes of the literary establishment," Andrew Sarris has remarked. "Such discredit is often unjustified even on literary grounds simply because many directors decline to take credit for collaborating on the writing of their films," or are simply not granted screen credit even when it is clearly deserved.

Commenting wryly on the legend promoted by film critics such as Pauline Kael that film directors too often seek to usurp a screen writer's credit, Russell recalls, "The only Hollywood writer I ever worked with, in fact, stole my credit. When the script came back from the printers with his name, and his alone, emblazoned all over the place, I naturally objected. 'But I did write it, Ken,' he protested. 'OK, so you dictated it; but I was the guy who typed it all out.' "

By consistently adapting the material which he films to his own personal vision and directorial style Russell has created his own world on film, a world that is no less uniquely his own because he has created it with the aid of various collaborators. Welcome, then, to the world of Ken Russell.

Acknowledgments

FIRST OF ALL, I am most grateful to Ken Russell, who not only discussed his films with me but arranged for me to see his early and more inaccessible films, and also corresponded with me about his work and has allowed me to quote from these letters which cover almost a decade.

I would also like to single out the following people among those who gave me their help:

Shirley Russell, who worked with Ken as costume designer over the last quarter of a century, and in the ten years I have been acquainted with them both has recalled many anecdotes about the making of the various television and feature films.

Dick Bush, who photographed seven TV and feature films for Ken Russell; Harry Benn, who produced several Russell features; Robert Littman, Russell's agent; Norman Swallow and Anthony Ham of Granada-TV; Patrick Sheehan of the Motion Picture Section of the Library of Congress; Jeremy Boulton of the National Film Archive of the British Film Institute; Charles Cooper of Contemporary Films, London; and film scholar Leo Murray for his careful reading of the typescript.

The stills reproduced in this book come from Ken Russell's own collection as well as from Granada-TV, United Artists, and BBC-TV.

Portions of this book appeared in a totally different form in the following publications:

"The Early Films" in *Ken Russell,* copyright 1976 by Simon and Schuster, reprinted with permission of the publisher; "Ken Russell," *Film Comment,* Fall 1970, copyright 1970 by Film Comment Publishing Company, and used with permission of the Film Society of Lincoln Center, all rights reserved; "Fact, Fantasy, and the Films of Ken Russell," *Journal of*

*   *   *

This book is for John Baxter.

Chronology

1927 Ken Russell born Henry Kenneth Alfred Russell in Southampton, England, July 3.

1941 Becomes a cadet at the Royal Naval College at Pangbourne and later joins the Merchant Navy.

1945 Released from naval service after a nervous breakdown and joins the RAF.

1948 Studies ballet after returning once more to civilian life and dances with several companies before he finally turns to photography as a profession.

1956 Makes his first noteworthy short, *Peep Show*, and converts to Roman Catholicism.

1957 Marries costume designer Shirley Ann Kingdon and works with her on photographic essays for *Illustrated, Picture Post,* and other magazines.

1958 Applies to BBC-TV to work in documentaries, submitting his short films as samples of his film work.

1959- Makes twenty short documentaries for the BBC arts
1962 program "Monitor."

1962 *Elgar* is telecast on November 11, bringing nationwide attention.

1963 Directs his first feature film, *French Dressing*.

1965 *The Debussy Film* is telecast on May 18, his last major biographical documentary for "Monitor" before it ceases production in June.

1966 *Isadora Duncan: The Biggest Dancer in the World*, his first major biographical telefilm for the "Omnibus" TV series, for which he makes the balance of his BBC films, is telecast September 22.

1967 *Billion Dollar Brain*, his second feature film; *Dante's*

Inferno, on the life of Dante Gabriel Rossetti, telecast December 22.

1968 *Song of Summer*, about the last years of Frederick Delius, telecast September 15.

1969 *Women in Love*, his third feature film, brings worldwide acclaim.

1970 *The Dance of the Seven Veils: A Comic Strip in Seven Episodes on the life of Richard Strauss*, prompts a furor after it is telecast on February 15, after which he leaves the BBC to work exclusively in feature films.

1970 *The Music Lovers*, based on the life of Tchaikovsky.

1971 *The Devils*; *The Boy Friend*.

1972 *Savage Messiah*, about sculptor Henri Gaudier.

1974 *Mahler*.

1975 *Tommy*; *Lisztomania*, suggested by the life of Franz Liszt.

1977 *Valentino*.

1978 Returns to television to make *Clouds of Glory*, a two-part series about the Lake Poets (Wordsworth and Coleridge), for Granada-TV, broadcast in two parts on July 9 and 16.

1

Getting Started: The Early Films

THE NAME of the London pub where I was to meet Ken Russell for what turned out to be the first of many interviews was the Intrepid Fox, located in downtown London near the dubbing theater where he was supervising the final editing of *The Music Lovers*. It was the spring of 1970 and Russell, at forty-two, had just burst into prominence on the international film scene with the worldwide release of *Women in Love*. American filmgoers wondered where this considerable talent had been keeping itself all these years; but British viewers were not the least bit surprised by the creativity and craftsmanship which Russell displayed in the film, since for a decade they had been treated to the series of excellent television films which he had made for the BBC.

When Russell appeared punctually at noon in a brown business suit with brass buttons, he seemed wary of meeting me, probably because American interest in his work was such a recent phenomenon that he had not met many American film writers. In any event, I was certainly wary of meeting him, since only a few days earlier his bizarre biographical telefilm on Richard Strauss had touched off a storm of controversy among television watchers and music lovers alike. Yet the man whose Strauss film had just been denounced in Parliament as an assault on the composer's life and work and on viewers' sensibilities as well turned out to be an engaging conversationalist who could discuss his TV and cinema work as dispassionately as if it had all been done by someone else.

What was supposed to be a lunch-hour interview ended at 3:00 P.M. when the bar closed for its afternoon recess. As he took leave of me, Russell said that he had enjoyed discussing his work with me. "Give me a couple of whiskeys and I'll waf-

23

*uthor Gene Phillips, Ken Russell and his wife Shirley
elebrate the completion of a film (credit: Metropolitan
hoto Service).*

fle on till closing time," he said with a wink. "I hope you can
make some sense out of my ramblings." Among his "ramblings" was a brief account of his youth and his initial interest in
movies.

Henry Kenneth Alfred Russell was born in the seaside port
of Southampton, England, on July 3, 1927. His father worked
in a shoe store, and young Ken would accompany his mother
to the movies while his father was busy in the shop. At other
times the lad, who had few childhood friends and who did not
even fraternize much with his younger brother, Raymond,
would sit alone and create a fantasy world of his own which of
course was stimulated by the films he had seen.

The young man who was to grow up to make a score of
period films hated the first historical movie he ever saw, the
Russian *Don Quixote* with Chaliapin, which he remembers as
"threadbare, corny, undramatic, and boring." At age twelve
Russell received a second-hand movie projector for Christmas,
along with a pile of old silent movies. Somewhat prophetically
the projector burst into flames one day while he was showing
a film—a forecast that the young Russell would grow up to ig-
nite movie screens with images of his own. Before his little
projector burned out, however, it had introduced him to Chaplin's shorts and to Max Fleischer's cartoons.

But it was the films of Germany's Golden Age of Silent
Cinema which were a real revelation to the youngster; he
would run Fritz Lang's *Die Nibelungen* and *Metropolis* over
and over again and be dazzled anew by their stark visual
power. Later, at boarding school, Russell made regular trips to
the local cinema, where he fell in love with musicals in general and those starring Dorothy Lamour in particular. At four-
teen Russell became a cadet at the Royal Naval College at
Pangbourne, where he produced an annual talent show that
included such highlights as a chorus of cadets doing a Carmen
Miranda number in drag, inspired by one of the many musical
films which he broke bounds to see in the nearby town. Also
while at Pangbourne, Russell made his first short film, with a
borrowed camera.

But his hopes of becoming a famous film director temporar-
ily vanished at the age of seventeen when Russell went to sea
as an apprentice sixth officer on a voyage to the South Seas.
"My dreams of finding a dusky native girl in a sarong on a

Pacific atoll were also dashed," he says, "when I learned that the ship was bound nonstop for Sydney, Australia." The romantic view of life at sea that Russell had garnered from those Dorothy Lamour and Carmen Miranda musicals about sailors visiting enchanted isles simply did not materialize in real life; in addition Russell grew more and more disaffected from navy life because of the rigid discipline that it imposed. Finally, after suffering a nervous breakdown, he was discharged at the end of World War II.

After he refused to join his father in the shoe shop, his parents declined to support their son, now in his late teens; and so he drifted into the RAF as an electrician for two years. Not surprisingly, he found the air force no more congenial than the navy had been. But, with the encouragement of a friend who was keen on ballet, Russell's interest in classical music, especially ballet scores, flourished.

When he returned once more to civilian life, he cast about for some type of career in the arts that would enable him to avoid settling for a drab job in an office or factory. By 1948 he had tentatively decided to try ballet as a profession. With some financial help from his parents (who were now reconciled to their wayward boy), he moved to London, where he got a job in an art gallery by day and attended classes in a third-rate ballet school by night. "But I never became a good dancer," he now concedes. "After working as a chorus boy in a tatty touring company of *Annie Get Your Gun*, as an actor in a shabby provincial acting troupe which went bankrupt in a few weeks, and at other ignoble jobs, I gave up the stage—or rather the stage gave me up."

It was about this time that Russell read H. S. Ede's *Savage Messiah*, the biography of the struggling young sculptor Henri Gaudier, who became the subject of Russell's 1972 film of that name. "This story about someone around my own age at the time," he says, "totally down and out but struggling onward nevertheless, gave me the courage to keep going, if not as a dancer or actor, then in some other art form. I was impressed by Gaudier's conviction that somehow or other there was a spark in the core of him that was personal to him, which was worth turning into something that could be appreciated by others. I wanted to find that spark in myself and exploit it for that reason."

Movies, Russell's first love, still remained a dream; the industry did not feel that he was suitably qualified since, as he says, his sole qualifications were "ten thousand films seen, plus the desire to make one of my own." He decided therefore to take up photography because he felt that it could eventually lead to filmmaking, a feeling shared by his father, who continued to give him a helping hand. "At twenty-six I must have been the oldest student in London learning the basics of photography," he remembers. "But I became fairly accomplished at it by photographing Shirley, whom I met at this time, while we were both studying at Walthamstow Technical College and Art School."

Shirley Ann Kingdon, who was to become Ken Russell's wife and costume designer, was studying fashion design while he studied photography. She was making clothes and Ken was photographing them in the hope that they could get some pictures into *Vogue*, but the fashions which Shirley designed were thought to be too far out for the conservative Fifties. "Besides," Russell adds, "I was not a magazine editor's idea of what a fashion photographer should look like. It wasn't fashionable in the 1950s for a fashion photographer to wear a

Young Ken Russell as a London sidewalk interviewer (1956)
(credit: The Last Picture Frock).

bright sport shirt and denim trousers. You were expected to wear a Bond Street suit with a white carnation in the lapel. I couldn't even afford the carnation." So Ken did freelance work for *Illustrated, Picture Post,* and other magazines, while Shirley worked for various London fashion houses as a designer. This helped finance a trio of amateur short films which eventually would enable Russell to land a job at BBC-TV.

Peep Show (1956)

The first of these amateur films was called *Peep Show.* It is significant that, since so much of his later work would deal with the struggles of the artist, this beginning film would be about two different kinds of purveyors of illusion. The first type is a group of con men who pose as disabled veterans to beg on the streets of London; the other are genuine performers, a pair of strolling players who do a pantomime routine in the street.

Because the film was made on a stringent budget of about $200, Russell made a virtue of necessity by designing the picture in the style of a primitive silent film. The movie was shot silent, and a pianola score was added to give the flavor of the nickelodeons. The dialogue titles, moreover, were chalked on sidewalks and fences.

Peep Show opens with the graduation ceremonies of the Bogus Beggars' Academy, where the surly looking "headmaster" is putting his latest batch of graduates through their paces to insure that they are ready to take to the streets. He says, "I'll teach you how to limp properly," and then kicks one of them in the shins. Meanwhile, three alumni who are busy practicing their trade on a London sidewalk discover that their business is falling off because pedestrians throw their spare change over a fence at something transpiring on the other side. The boss comes to look into the matter; and, because neither he nor his men can find a spare knothole to look through, all four leap over the fence.

They find a father and daughter team doing a pantomime routine: the old man is a magician who enacts the role of master of a life-size doll. The old man takes the doll out of a huge box and winds it up. The doll begins to play a drum and do a dance while the old man joins in with his clarinet. Their act

ends with the doll locking its master into the box and collapsing against it, completely unwound.

The four men carry off the box, release the old man, and
force him to hand over all his coins. One of the group balks at
his cohorts' mistreatment of the elderly gentleman, and the
rest respond by knocking him cold and making off once more
with the old man. The old man's daughter, who has witnessed
these events, revives the reformed con man, and together they
pursue the others. But the girl's father, it turns out, can take
care of himself: like a Pied Piper, he lures the four crooks with
his clarinet tune into a river, where they float off on the doll
box, which they have been forced to convert into a raft. Father
and daughter are reunited and, together with the converted
beggar, they dance off—not into the sunset but into the mist of
a typically foggy London day.

The crucial character, then, is the young man who begins by
utilizing the art of illusion in his dishonest masquerade as a
blind beggar and ends by joining the genuine practitioners of
the art of illusion who seek to lighten the lives of others with
their entertaining pantomimes. One is reminded of Luis
Buñuel's remark that "the cinema is a dangerous and wonderful instrument if a free spirit uses it," dangerous only if used
irresponsibly. "There are always some men who will try to
express their inner world, to convey it to others through the
medium of the film, which is above all a marvelous tool for
artistic creation." There is no doubt that from the time of his
first movie Ken Russell wanted to take his place among those
free spirits, symbolized at the end of *Peep Show* by the exuberant trio disappearing over the horizon.

The magician-father was played by a friend of Russell's from
the north of England who lived at the same boarding house as
he did at the time. This young man happened to be a Roman
Catholic, and he interested Russell in joining the Church during the period when *Peep Show* was being shot. Just before
shooting was completed he was converted to Roman Catholicism, as was Shirley.

"I was ripe for conversion," Russell recalls; he had been
genuinely moved by, among other things, his friend's simple
and firm belief that Christ was mystically present in the bread
and wine of the Communion service of the Mass, "the most
mind-shattering thing that had ever struck me." In addition,

he was deeply impressed by the nuns at the convent where he went for instructions in the Faith; they worked with the sick and the poor, and Russell found their dedication a real inspiration.

"When I was young I really didn't know where I was going," he comments; "but as soon as I came into the Faith my work, my philosophy gained direction. I began to think more clearly, to see much further. The faith taught me that there is no easy road in life. I realized that I could survive anything in my quest to fulfill my potential as a person and as an artist. I am a lapsed Catholic now; I think one of the reasons that I left the Church is that I couldn't live up to it, I wasn't good enough to continue. Nevertheless I think my films are an intense affirmation of my faith; almost all of my films are Catholic in outlook: films about love, faith, sin, guilt, forgiveness, and redemption—films that could only have been made by a Catholic." Significantly, all of these themes can be found implicitly in Russell's next short film, *Amelia and the Angel*, the most seminal of Russell's early works.

Amelia and the Angel (1957)

Soon after becoming a Catholic convert, Russell married Shirley, and they went on working at photography and design in order to finance their short films, one of which they knew would eventually bring them recognition. For their next cinematic venture they decided to do a little movie that would be a kind of religious valentine to their recently found religious faith; indeed, the credits of the movie are enshrined in a lacey border that resembles a greeting card.

Russell visited the Catholic Film Institute in London, which at that time provided an information service on current films for Catholic subscribers and also distributed 16mm films to Catholic schools and institutions. Russell accordingly inquired whether or not they would be interested in backing his film. As he soon discovered, the office was primarily interested in renting to its constituents short films that were mainly of an instructional nature and declined to finance *Amelia*. But the young film enthusiast named Anthony Evans, who virtually ran the institute singlehandedly, was excited about Russell's projected film, and offered to work on the script and otherwise help out in any way that he could. As always Shirley Russell provided the costumes, and set about touring bargain basements and thrift shops to find material that she could transform into cheaply made costumes that would not look cheaply made, an ability which she has perfected in the intervening years.

Mercedes Quadros as Amelia in *Amelia and the Angel* (credit: British National Film Archive).

To play the key role of Amelia, Russell enlisted nine-year-old Mercedes Quadros, the daughter of the ambassador from Uruguay to England at the time. Mercedes consented to play the part, provided that Russell was willing to take her on auto tours of London at breakneck speed, presumably because she was bored with riding in slow-moving limousines. "She loved the rides," Russell remembers, "and all the while I was wondering if we would be arrested or killed before the film was over. Apart from that one rather unconventional request, however, Mercedes was very accommodating while we were shooting the picture. I got a letter from her years later in which she said that making that movie was one of the most memorable experiences of her life. I still wonder if it is those rides round the city rather than appearing in the film that she remembers best."

Amelia and the Angel opens with a close-up of a polython, the forerunner of the modern phonograph, which played perforated metal discs. The sound track of the movie is made up of classical and popular themes played on such a machine, and on similar mechanical music boxes. The camera pans from the ancient gramophone to a group of little girls dressed in angelic attire circling around a large rehearsal hall under the direction of their middle-aged teacher, Miss May. "Five girls in a play," the narrator intones, "and this is the story of Amelia, the least angelic of them all." The girls depart after their rehearsal concludes, and for a moment the large room is empty. Then the door at the far end of the hall opens cautiously, and Amelia reappears. Stealthily she snatches her pair of wings, of which she is particularly proud, and disappears through the doorway.

"She knew it was wrong," the narrator whispers confidentially, "but there she was taking the wings home to show her mother, even though Miss May had warned the girls that if anything happened to their wings they would not find another pair this side of heaven." Amelia rides home on the underground, and as she gets off the train and scrambles through the crowd on the platform Russell photographs the scene from a low angle, showing how the world looks from the waist-high point of view of a child, allowing the handheld camera to be jostled in the same way that Amelia is.

Her jealous little brother makes off with the wings and frolics with them in a nearby park, only to return home with them torn and tattered. As might be expected, Amelia is inconsolable. Through her tears she studies two religious pictures on her bedroom wall: one is an angel and the other a saintly artist holding a palette. She breathes a silent prayer and then runs out of the house and down the street, hoping that somewhere this side of heaven she can beg, borrow, or buy with the little money that she has a new pair of wings. The camera tracks laterally beside her as she runs from stall to stall in a sidewalk market, nearly frantic with fear that she will not be able to appear in the school play.

Finally, Amelia spies a young woman carrying a pair of angel wings into a tenement. The little girl timidly walks up the stone steps to the porch. The camera shifts to inside the house as Amelia pushes the door open, giving the effect of an iris-in, which reveals the child framed in the doorway. As she

climbs in silhouette the shadowy steps to the dark at the top of
the stairs, the scene takes on an unearthly, otherworldly atmosphere.

She goes into a room bathed in light where the young woman, now dressed as a Botticelli angel, is posing for an artist.
The pair are the embodiment of the two holy pictures which
Amelia had prayed before back in her room at home. Both look
down benignly at Amelia as she explains her plight. Without a
word the painter climbs up an endless ladder out of frame, and
after a moment climbs back down into view carrying a pair of
angel wings for Amelia. (Just how high we are to infer that he
had to soar to secure the extra wings for Amelia is a question
that Russell prefers not to answer—in order to leave such
speculations about the meaning of his little allegory to the
moviegoer.)

Amelia laughs exultantly as she runs out of the building and
disappears in the distance, holding the wings high above her
head, and the film ends. The girl has experienced guilt and
sorrow for disobeying Miss May, and as a result she has received a kind of symbolic absolution which is concretized in
the granting of her prayer that she find another pair of wings.
Here for the first time, then, Russell deals with sin, guilt, forgiveness, and redemption—themes which will become much
more apparent in his mature work.

Lourdes (1958)

It occurred to Russell that if he wanted to convince the BBC
that he was capable of doing conventional documentaries as
well as imaginative allegories like *Amelia*, he had better shoot
a garden-variety documentary more along the lines of the kind
of thing which the BBC was accustomed to airing. Accordingly
he and Tony Evans flew to Lourdes to shoot a documentary
about the famed shrine to the Blessed Virgin Mary and the
hordes of pilgrims that come there from all over the world.

When it was completed, Tony Evans convinced his
superiors to distribute the film through the Catholic Film Institute rental library, Russell recalls, "but minus the sequence
satirizing the commercial side of Lourdes, with its miles of
rosary beads, millions of plaster statues, and records for sale."
This sequence has been restored, however, in the version of

the film now circulated in Britain by Contemporary Films, and is the most imaginative segment in the entire film. "This is also Lourdes," says the narrator wryly, as the endless lines of statues of the Blessed Mother and of Bernadette pass before the camera as if they were on an assembly-line conveyor belt.

The overall tone of the film, nonetheless, radiates genuine respect for the devotion of the pilgrims, even though Russell's satire on the "carnival" aspect of the shrine, with its gaudy neon lights at night reminding one for a moment of Las Vegas, would surface twenty years later in *Tommy*.

Russell submitted *Lourdes* and *Amelia* to Norman Swallow, at that time assistant head of films at BBC-TV, who in turn had *Amelia* screened for Huw Wheldon, supervisor of the bi-weekly "Monitor" arts program, presumably because *Amelia* was the more inventive of the two films—although Russell had explicitly shot *Lourdes* to demonstrate his ability to do a routine documentary. Wheldon found *Amelia* both romantic and eccentric, but also imaginative and free of clichés. After interviewing Russell, Wheldon decided to have him replace John Schlesinger, who was moving on to feature films, on "Monitor."

"I started on 'Monitor' by doing a series of short films on a variety of subjects ranging from pop art to folk dancing, from the guitar craze to brass bands at a miners' picnic," Russell recalls.

The Miners' Picnic (1960)

Russell's evocation of life in the mining towns in the north of England is indicative of his early BBC short documentaries in the way that he manages to pack so much significant detail into a mere quarter of an hour. Each of the coal mines in the district has its own band, and these bands compete for first prize in the music competition held every year as part of the miners' annual picnic. Russell implies how this leisure-time activity of playing in the band lightens the load of a miner's life by cutting from the band members playing their hearts out on parade to the same men deep in the pits shoveling coal, with the band music continuing on the sound track all the while. In another telling shot the camera pans from the tuba player's face, as he puffs away during a band rehearsal, down to his grimy fingernails, suggesting the arduous work from which the band provides a respite.

The short film concludes with some of the band members riding the merry-go-round at the fair grounds, a beautiful metaphor for the grinding repetition of their lives, from which the activities of the miners' picnic provide a welcome interruption.

The miner-bandsman who narrates the film remarks in the course of his voice-over commentary, "I still think that even if some of the collieries do close, the bands will continue." "Unfortunately he was wrong," says Russell today. "When I went back to the same area to shoot the mining scenes in *Women in Love* less than ten years later, most of the collieries had disappeared, and most of the bands had gone with them." Russell's nostalgia for the passing of the old order is reflected in another film that he made in this period, his first full-length documentary, *A House in Bayswater*, which Russell's fellow BBC veteran John Schlesinger still believes to be a minor masterpiece among Russell's work.

A House in Bayswater (1960)

The thirty-minute film begins with a shot of the scaffolding of a modern skyscraper rising against the sky, followed by a shot of the Edwardian mansion that once stood in its place. In its last years the venerable old house had been converted into an apartment building (where Russell himself lived at one point); and the durable old landlady takes the viewer on a tour of the place as it was when it was still inhabited before the wrecker's ball destroyed the edifice to make way for a new office building. "A lot of people have passed through here, but at the moment we have a nice crowd in," she says as she goes from apartment to apartment introducing the viewer to the tenants, which include a photographer, a painter, a retired ballet dancer who still gives lessons to aspiring young dancers, and a former lady's maid who worked for a wealthy family in New York in the Twenties.

It is the elderly women—the landlady, the retired dancer, and the ex-servant—who are of special interest in the film because they, like the house, seem to be enriched by their identification with the past. But the trio of ladies are also wise enough to know that life goes on, and that one cannot live completely in the past if one is to survive in the present.

Helen May, the former ballerina, sees her young pupils as an extension of herself; and she equivalently carries on her career in them. This is clearly implied in the sequence in which one of her pupils comes for a lesson and practices a routine that Ms. May had done on the New York stage in the Twenties, and even wears a dancing costume modeled on the one which Ms. May herself is pictured as wearing in a vintage poster hanging on her living-room wall. The dance, the costume, and the music on the old phonograph which accompanies the girl's number are all out-of-date, and all the more touching for that. What one admires most in Ms. May is her undiminished spirit, which she communicates to her neophyte ballerina along with the dancing lessons.

Russell symbolically toasts Ms. May's indomitable spirit and the inspiration which she is for her young pupil in a fantasy sequence (one of the very first Russell introduced into a documentary): Ms. May, suitcase in hand, and the girl are battling against a strong wind which carries them out through the front door of the apartment building. This dream vision, photographed in slow motion and soft focus, is a premonition of the inevitable destruction of the old house in favor of the new office building that will replace it. These dauntless old people like Ms. May have learned to come to terms with the past and to cope with the present; and they must now face the future with equanimity as they are once more uprooted and forced to move on. And one knows that somehow they will.

"During this period I also made some short films on living artists such as the poet John Betjeman and playwright Shelagh Delaney," Russell recalls; "and when there were no more live artists left, we turned to making somewhat longer films about dead artists such as Prokofiev. At first we were only allowed to use still photographs and newsreel footage of these subjects, but eventually we sneaked in the odd hand playing the piano and the odd back walking through a door. By the time a couple of years had gone by, these boring little factual accounts of the artists had evolved into evocative films of an hour or more which used real actors to impersonate the historical figures that we were portraying."

Prokofiev (1961)

Portrait of a Soviet Composer: Prokofiev was Russell's first biographical film for the BBC on an artist already deceased, and with it began his attempts to insinuate elements of dramatic re-creation into a film that otherwise depended on photos, old feature footage, and newsreels to tell its story. The movie opens with two pairs of hands playing a piano duet; the hands are meant to represent those of Prokofiev's mother and of the boy himself. The mother's hands disappear and the lad continues to play alone, a symbol of how Prokofiev's mother encouraged his early interest in music and of how the boy went on to progress on his own.

Sometimes the composer's music on the sound track is meant to complement the images, as when his score for the Eisenstein film *Alexander Nevsky* is employed as accompaniment for the newsreel shots of Russian troops going into battle in World War II, a reminder that Prokofiev's score for the film was often employed to boost Russian morale during the war. At other times Prokofiev's music is paired with images to which it serves as an ironic contrast, as when footage of an exuberant postwar May Day parade is yoked to the somber strains of his Sixth Symphony, which was banned at the time because the authorities found it out of touch with the optimistic temper of the times.

These sequences in the film, while suggesting the imagination which Russell was already bringing to his documentaries, were still well within the realm of conventional documentary filmmaking. Russell ran into trouble, however, when he sought to employ an actor to portray Prokofiev even in a fleeting image on the screen. BBC executives rejected this notion as "cheating," but grudgingly allowed a single shot of Prokofiev reflected in a pool, only because the muddy water was murky enough to make the actor's face barely distinguishable.

The irony about the BBC's refusal to allow the reenactment of any of the episodes in Prokofiev's life in the film is that the footage which Russell used of the storming of the Winter Palace during the Russian Revolution was not in fact from newsreels but from the re-creation of the event in Eisenstein's silent film *October*. In the course of making *Prokofiev* Russell had nevertheless made some inroads against BBC policy, and he would make further advances along the same path in his next biographical movie.

Elgar (1962)

Elgar was the watershed documentary in Russell's progress toward making biographical films that would be a blend of documentary and drama, and which would come to be known as biopics. For a start, Wheldon agreed to have not just one actor impersonate the great English composer in the film but four, each representing Elgar at a different stage of his life; but they were not to speak a word of dialogue. This prohibition proved no handicap for Russell on this particular film, however, since he worked up a beautiful series of visuals that added depth and dimension to Wheldon's spoken narration and the musical score.

In one sequence Russell depicts the loneliness which Elgar and his wife experienced—because Elgar's lower-class Roman Catholic background precluded their being socially accepted—by picturing them in a rowboat in the middle of an isolated lake. Later Russell implies the emotional support that Elgar's wife provided for him in the bleak years in which his music went without recognition by another telling visual symbol. As Elgar sits composing at a table in a gloomy room, his wife enters and turns up the gas lamp, filling the room with light and warmth, a luminous image of her role as angel of consolation in this dark period of his life.

But the visual image that captured the imagination of the mass audience is that of Elgar as a lad galloping across his beloved Malvern Hills on horseback to the strains of one of Elgar's lushest compositions for string orchestra. Indeed, one of Elgar's biographers has hazarded that few people who have seen Russell's film can hear the composer's *Introduction and Allegro for Strings* without its conjuring up the vision of that boy astride his white pony.

Russell provides visual continuity in the film by presenting a variation of this image at two later points in the film. As a young adult Elgar is shown bicycling over the lanes of the Malvern Hills after he has returned to his boyhood home in the wake of official rejection by the British musical establishment in London; and finally Elgar is seen in the autumn of his

Ken Russell directing the BBC-TV film *Elgar* (credit: BBC-TV).

life motoring through the hills once more as he goes back to his roots to end his days.

Wheldon and Russell had thus reached a working agreement about the introduction of dramatic re-enactment into biographical documentaries, but they disagreed on other issues. Russell projected Elgar's consternation about his Pomp and Circumstance March being used as a patriotic marching song to send soldiers off to die at the front in World War I by accompanying the march in his film with newsreel shots of wounded and maimed troops dying ignominiously amid the mud and barbed wire of the battlefield. Wheldon objected to this sequence as editorializing on Russell's part, and they compromised by cutting the sequence's running time exactly in half.

The Elgar film was well received, but Russell personally was not satisfied with it. "I pictured Elgar as having his ups and downs and not being recognized as a great composer until late in life," he explains. "But basically it was a sentimental, romantic film, showing Elgar galloping across the Malvern Hills on horseback in the early morning and so on. The film was all too lovely, like a TV commercial for the Malvern Hills! I was perhaps too much in love with the man's music to see what really produced it. If I were to remake the film, I would be far truer to the man and his struggle than I was the first time. I would show the darker side of his life as well as the lyrical, colorful side." He would, for example, include Elgar's obsession with suicide (mentioned only in passing in the original film), and his somewhat ambiguous relationship with his publisher and friend Jaeger (not mentioned at all in original movie).

As recently as July 1976 Russell was trying to finance a remake of his Elgar film, this time as a feature. He wrote in a letter at the time, "I, an Englishman, had to go to Paris to try to raise money from a French producer to make a film on the greatest British composer of all time since I couldn't get financing in England."[1] That deal fell through, but Russell still cherishes the hope of rejuvenating the project. "I still love Elgar," he says; "but this time I would want to depict the complete man, 'warts and all,' as they say."

Although *Elgar* went on to become one of the most popular single TV programs ever screened in Britain and gained Russell nationwide attention, at the time of its premiere he saw it only as a stepping stone to making the kind of imaginative biopics which he had had in mind all along. He was endeavoring to evolve a new concept of film biography that would liberate that genre from the conventions of the old-fashioned movie biographies of the past; and the success of the Elgar film at last prompted the BBC to give him the opportunity to do just that.

2

The Past as Present: The Biographical Television Films

"MY FIRST TV DOCUMENTARIES coincided with the accepted textbook idea of what a documentary should be," Russell explains. "You were supposed to extol the great artists and their work, and this is what I did for the most part in *Elgar*. Finally I decided to dispel the preconceived idea of what a documentary had to be by presenting the life of a great artist in a way that showed how he transcended his own personal problems and weaknesses in creating great art. Showing the personal struggles out of which an artist's work grew is more of a tribute to him than making believe that he was some sort of saint sitting quietly in his studio creating masterpieces. I took a more controversial approach in my TV documentaries about such artists as Dante Gabriel Rossetti, Frederick Delius, Isadora Duncan, and Richard Strauss. In all of these biographies I tried to condense the essense of an artist's life and work into the brief span of a telefilm."

Bartók (1964)

Russell's first attempt at painting an unglamorized portrait of an artist was his film on the Hungarian composer Béla Bartók, who died in exile in New York City at the end of the Second World War. The BBC allowed Russell for the first time to use an actor in close shots (and not just distance shots as in *Elgar*) to enact the role of the composer—although Russell was still not permitted to have the actor speak any lines of dialogue. Yet the concession about close-ups brought Russell one step closer to his goal of fully dramatizing an artist's life in a biopic.

Bartók is pictured as a solitary old man sitting alone in a

43

sparely furnished little room in New York in 1942 as he recalls his past life and his musical career. In contrast to this subdued setting, to which Russell frequently returns as a frame of reference throughout the film, the director has orchestrated several scenes of violence and terror from Bartók's ballet and opera scores.

Russell dramatizes a scene from Bartók's ballet *The Miraculous Mandarin*, for example, that is really quite devastating. A prostitute is discovered in a stark hotel room, enticing a young man on the street below to join her. As they prepare to make love, a black-gloved hand slams over his mouth, and the camera pulls back to show her two accomplices beating and robbing the luckless youth, much to her sadistic delight.

The young man escapes from his captors and runs out of the building and through a shadowy passageway until he reaches a dead end. He hopelessly turns to confront the thugs who have been in hot pursuit of him all the while. Bartók's music from the ballet continues on the sound track as the two ruffians brutally club their victim, and Russell cuts to policemen clubbing rioters in the streets of Hungary at the end of World War I when the new Hungarian nation was struggling to be born. This brilliant blend of music and editing makes the point that in his musical compositions like *The Miraculous Mandarin* ballet Bartók mirrored the horror and brutality of the real world, which was scarred by two world wars during his lifetime.

Bartók was fundamentally a deeply shy, private person who felt woefully estranged from the hostile, chaotic world which he saw all around him as he lived out his life exiled in the hectic, overcrowded atmosphere of wartime New York. His inability to adjust to the big city's fast pace, aggressiveness, and noise is epitomized in the shots of a jammed subway train, whose clattering racket drowns out even the crashing chords of his own music heard on the sound track, and on which he is trying to concentrate in his own mind as he rides along in the hot and dirty train.

His alienation from the world at large was increased by the persistent rejection by critics and concertgoers alike of what they termed the "monstrous modernism" of his music. Bartók hated having to expose his highly personal music to the pitiless scrutiny of unsympathetic strangers; and Russell projects Bartók's excruciating sense of alienation and isolation, because of the perpetual rejection of his work, by photographing him on what seems to be an endless descending subway escalator, standing between people who glare at him impassively, while yet more anonymous strangers are continually borne toward him on an ascending escalator.

In harmony with Russell's intention to create biopics that depict the personal problems and struggles out of which an artist's work is born, he does not hesitate to present Bartók as a withdrawn, desperately melancholy man whose music provided for him a refuge from a cruel and uncomprehending world. Thus Bartók found some degree of solace in his last months of life in composing his Concerto for Orchestra, which was inspired by the traditional folk music of his native Hungary. The music of the Concerto is appropriately accompanied in the last sequence of the film by shots of Hungarian peasants which are crisply edited to the tempo of the music, and which serve to provide a moving conclusion to a somber and touching film.

Bartók is a fairly accomplished film, considering that Russell's budget forced him to rely a great deal on newsreels and stock footage for his visuals, though not to the same extent that he did on *Prokofiev*. Anyone familiar with London will marvel in seeing how Russell has made excellent use of his limited opportunities for location shooting. In *The Miraculous Mandarin* sequence, for instance, the frightened youth is pursued through an eerie tunnel that is really the underground pedestrian crosswalk in the Tottenham Court Road subway station in the heart of downtown London.

All of the films which Russell made for television were done on tiny budgets; and Russell therefore had to tax his artistic ingenuity to find ways of creating the atmosphere of a historical setting when, as he says, "I couldn't afford to have period costumes for more than six extras. I had no way to create nineteenth-century Paris in my film on Debussy, for example." Russell solved the latter problem by building his film on Debussy around a group of actors who are making a TV movie about the composer; in this way he was able to set the film virtually in the present.

The Debussy Film (1965)

The concept of *The Debussy Film* first occurred to Russell as a possibility for a feature film, and he worked out a script with writer Melvyn Bragg, who was also associated with "Monitor" and who was to collaborate several more times with Russell in the years to come. After their script was judged to be too sophisticated for a theatrical feature, it was accepted by the BBC. The ingenious format of showing a TV crew making the film-within-a-film of Debussy's life also enabled Russell to get round the BBC's restriction, still in force from the days of *Elgar* and *Bartók*, that he could use actors to re-enact episodes from the subject's life only if they spoke no lines, lest viewers be "cheated" into believing that they were seeing newsreels of real people instead of watching actors impersonating them. In the script of *Debussy* the actors were clearly identified as actors playing the various historical figures in the film.

Russell and Bragg devised several scenes in which the actor playing Debussy in the film-within-a-film (Oliver Reed) discusses aspects of the composer's life and personality with the director of the film-within-a-film (Vladek Sheybal), who also plays Debussy's mentor Pierre Louys in the movie which they are making. In this fashion Russell is able to illuminate the ambiguities of Debussy's character, which in many ways was as elusive as his music. Since the relationship of the actor and the director making the film parallels that of Debussy and Louys in the film-within-a-film, it often does not matter whether these interchanges are between actor and director or between composer and mentor since the dynamics of their interaction is identical: the younger man is being challenged and inspired by the older man with more experience of life and art.

At other points in the film Russell draws additional parallels between the historical personages that are represented in the film-within-a-film and the relationships of the actors playing the roles. An outstanding example of this is the scene in which the actress playing Debussy's mistress Gaby demonstrates her lack of comprehension and interest in Debussy's music to the actor playing Debussy by reacting as negatively to one of Debussy's compositions as Gaby herself would have. During a cast party the actor playing Debussy plays a recording of Debussy's Danse Profane, and the actress playing Gaby cynically ridicules the piece by doing a striptease in time to the music.

In another scene Russell slyly satirizes the BBC's insistence that his biopics be factually accurate in every detail. The director of the film-within-a-film comments enthusiastically as he runs a slow-motion sequence for the cast in which Debussy and Gaby sensuously fondle a breastlike balloon to the accompaniment of Afternoon of a Faun, "They *did* play with balloons! I checked it!" Russell is convinced that no biographical film can ever capture the authentic essence of an artist's life or work, no matter how faithful it is to the official facts; and this is his way of saying so.

Russell's film also makes this point at the very beginning when the director coaches a young actor (played by Russell's son Xavier) to say to another onlooker as Debussy's funeral cortege passes in the rain, "It seems he was a musician." The director himself repeats this line at the very end of the film, the only explicit statement that the director is sure that he can make about Debussy. Like his counterpart in *The Debussy Film*, Russell as director has sought to show the viewer what he thinks of Debussy in images rather than to try to formulate his feelings in words, allowing the viewer to draw his own conclusions. Thus one of the last scenes in the film-within-a-film depicts Debussy surrounded by apparitions of the two women whom he had driven to attempted suicide; this is Russell's way of dramatizing rather than verbalizing what he considers to be Debussy's calloused disregard for the other people in his life.

Because of the implicit criticism of Debussy's behavior in the film, Huw Wheldon insisted that the biopic begin with a series of Louy's photographs of Debussy accompanied by a spoken statement assuring the television audience that they were about to see a film based on incidents in Debussy's life and incorporating direct quotations from Debussy himself. Despite these cautious statements that *The Debussy Film* was fundamentally a conventional biographical documentary, it was nothing of the sort. Russell had broken the BBC's taboo against directly dramatizing the life of an artist, and the way was now open for him to present the lives of other artists in future biopics in an even more imaginative and personal way than he had been allowed to do in the past.

The Debussy Film is therefore a transitional film for Russell, separating his earlier, more straightforward documentaries like *Prokofiev* and *Elgar* from his subsequent fully dramatized biopics. As such it is not as accomplished a work as the biopics to come would be; Russell was still feeling his way. Hence the structural framework of the film-within-a-film format is sometimes awkwardly managed. For example, Russell introduces a fantasy sequence built around Debussy's Festival Nocturne by simply having the director mutter that this particular Debussy selection is one of his personal favorites. The fantasy sequence which follows, with its stunningly photographed torchlight procession, has little relevance to the dramatic content of the overall film, in contrast to the Faun sequence just mentioned, in which Russell uses Debussy's erotic music to accompany a love scene between Debussy and Gaby.

Although *The Debussy Film* is somewhat flawed, in his next biopic Russell consolidated the advances which he had made since coming to the BBC in creating his own special brand of biographical documentary-drama.

Always on Sunday (1965)

Despite the fact that *Always on Sunday* is not one of Russell's more celebrated biopics, it is a remarkable work which deals in bittersweet terms with the life of Henri Rousseau, who retired from the French civil service after the death of his wife to devote himself to painting, an avocation which he heretofore had relegated to Sundays.

The genesis of this delightful film really goes back to a documentary about the contemporary Yorkshire painter James Lloyd, which Russell had done the previous year. The arresting simplicity of Lloyd's work reminded Russell of Rousseau's pristinely primitive style, and he therefore asked Lloyd to play Rousseau in *Always on Sunday*. Although this film still relies heavily on narration (spoken by Oliver Reed), it is nonetheless the first completely dramatized biopic which Russell had made for the BBC, in which the artist's life was re-enacted completely by actors. Lloyd's feeling of kinship for Rousseau, furthermore, enabled him to identify so totally with the role that he truly inhabits the part rather than plays it.

Russell distills the abiding condescension of the art world for Rousseau's unfashionably quaint paintings by the device of having the same pompous art critic (Bryan Pringle) and his girl friend show up at every exhibition that features a Rousseau work in order to ridicule the artist and his paintings. Rousseau's reaction to this negative response to his art is always the same: he stands impassively next to his painting with arms folded, radiating the serene confidence that he will have the last laugh. And indeed he will, though his vindication will not come until after he is dead. As Rousseau dies in the pauper's ward of a hospital, Oliver Reed ironically remarks, voice-over, that the Rousseau painting that hangs in the Museum of Modern Art in New York City is valued at one million dollars.

Yet the film is not bitter or morose. Rousseau himself is such a disarming man that it is his warm and human spirit, and not the mean-spiritedness of his detractors, which permeates the movie. In one scene he gallantly but ineptly proposes to a woman, assuring her that his dead wife won't mind if he remarries; and then he tries to ingratiate himself with her further by showing off his paintings to her. This turns out to be a real tactical error. As she peruses the legion of unsold pictures that crowd his tiny flat, her titters turn into guffaws, and finally uproarious laughter which is multiplied on the sound track into the chorus of critical derision that has always greeted Rousseau's work. She walks out, leaving him alone, yet surrounded by the work that is beloved to him if to no one else.

Repeatedly during the movie Rousseau is shown laboriously negotiating a wheelbarrow freighted with one of his huge canvases along the road to an exhibition, only to wheel it home again unsold. This shot becomes a touching metaphor for Rousseau's career as an artist: weighed down by indifference and rejection, he nonetheless carries on. It is fitting, then, that this shot appears one last time at film's end, for it represents Rousseau just the way we would like to remember him—as the loveable man and undaunted artist.

In *Always on Sunday* Russell proved that he had totally mastered this new form of dramatized biography which he had been gradually developing through several films. In his next biopic he would come up with one of the finest films which he has ever made in any genre.

Isadora Duncan: The Biggest Dancer in the World (1966)

Russell directed his television version of the life of Isadora Duncan two years before Karel Reisz made his feature film *The Loves of Isadora*. "Reisz's film version used most of the incidents in Isadora's life that I used," says Russell, "but I managed to tell her story with a little more economy in about half the time that his film runs." This is partially due to the fact that Russell begins his TV biopic by running through the whole of Isadora Duncan's life in a kind of kaleidoscopic newsreel. Russell is able thereby to give the audience a synopsis of her life that provides a frame of reference for the series of flashbacks that make up the balance of the film.

This opening prologue also encapsulates the image of Isadora Duncan (Vivian Pickles) as the public knew her, as a legendary figure whose life was as bizarre and devil-may-care as her art (see picture at the opening of this chapter). Then the film proceeds to portray Isadora as she really was, a tragic creature who remained fundamentally unfulfilled both as a person and as an artist. Russell suggests during the credits that life for Isadora was a contest by having her first name shouted out a letter at a time as if by cheerleaders at a football match; and the balance of the movie goes on to show that Isadora basically lost that contest.

The movie proper, after the prologue, is narrated by Sewell Stokes, who knew Isadora during her last days. The rights to his biography of her had been purchased by the producers of the Reisz film, but it occurred to Russell that the movie producers had not purchased Stokes's memory along with the rights to his book. Therefore Russell had Stokes recall anew for him many of the things that he knew about Isadora and had his remarks framed into the film's narration. Russell's desire for authenticity did not hamper his creative imagination, however. "Since Isadora's life was so pathetic, I wanted to lighten the material at times," he remembers. "For example I used the old Betty Hutton recording of 'The Sewing Machine' from the 1947 Hollywood film *The Perils of Pauline* on the sound track when Isadora was falling in love with Paris Singer, the sewing-machine manufacturer." Nevertheless Russell's *Isadora* has some darker moments which are not in Reisz's film. For instance, Russell indicates that Isadora's Russian husband, Yesenin, the only one of her several lovers that she ever married, was an epileptic and a kleptomaniac, further complicating their already tragic relationship.

Russell's budget would not permit his filming the episode in which Paris Singer brought a fifty-piece orchestra aboard his yacht to accompany Isadora's dancing on the deck, nor did he have the rights to the book in which the episode was mentioned. So Russell's fertile imagination concocted a visual equivalent for this incident in which Singer presents Isadora with an enormous gold box when she comes to live in his mansion. The sides of the box fall away to reveal six harpists who then accompany Isadora's dance. "That's a good example," Russell comments, "of finding a parallel incident which, although it cannot be as good as the truth, has some sort of flavor of the original."[1]

Russell shows Isadora's failure to communicate with the men in her life in equally inventive ways. He first shows her engaging in a shouting match with Singer while he is swimming in an indoor pool, and their voices bounce incomprehensibly off the tiled walls. Later he stages a quarrel between Isadora and Yesenin which is refereed by a hapless interpreter

Vivian Pickles as Isadora Duncan listens to an interpreter through whom she communicates with her Russian husband (credit: BBC-TV).

who must translate the mutual recriminations for the angry pair.

The director wins audience sympathy for his stubborn and eccentric heroine, however, by delineating her great love for children, first for her own little boy and girl, who are tragically drowned in an auto mishap; and then for her surrogate children, the hundreds of little girls for whom she conducts a ballet school. As a result we care for Isadora as a human being even while she increasingly takes refuge in drugs, alcohol, and gigolos in the course of her decline. The heavy makeup which she applies to conceal the ravages of age and dissipation of course makes her look all the more pathetic.

She is indeed very touching when she appears at a garden party in her honor late in her life and throws to the ground a floral bouquet that has been presented to her by a group of aspiring ballerinas as she utters the heartbreaking words, "I lay this wreath on the grave of my hopes." Her bitter reference to death foreshadows her demise, which follows soon after. To the ironic strains of "Thanks for the Buggy Ride" on the sound track, Isadora goes for a spin in a sports car with her latest male companion, and her long scarf catches in the spokes of one of the wheels of the speeding car, instantly strangling her to death.

The final, frantically wild car ride sums up how Isadora lived a fast life and burned herself out, while the dream-vision of a thousand of her "children" dancing to Beethoven's Choral Symphony which fills the screen for a moment vividly contrasts her dreams with the cruel reality of her life and death. One cannot but pity Isadora during the final fade-out, a close-up of her face in death, relentlessly photographed so as to highlight her excessive use of cosmetics, which gives to her visage the character of a grotesque mask. Russell would be somewhat less sympathetic to the subject of his next TV biopic, Dante Gabriel Rossetti.

Dante's Inferno (1967)

In *Dante's Inferno* Russell mingles fantasy with reality more than in any of his previous biopics in order to dramatize more forcefully the gap between objective truth and artistic illusion, as well as the way that the artist tries to improve one by the use of the other. This theme, which Russell touched upon in his earlier biopics, is most strikingly reflected in the present film in the contrast between Rossetti's wife, Lizzie, a none-too-bright ex-trollop (Judith Paris), as she is in real life and the way that Rossetti (Oliver Reed) enshrines her in his poetry and in his paintings.

We see this gap between Lizzie as she is and as Rossetti pictures her as she models for his painting of Joan of Arc. The plain, not very attractive girl is transformed on the canvas into a radiant and imposing figure. By the same token we hear Rossetti's voice on the sound track intone in rich, romantic accents a poem that he has dedicated to her, only to have his voice replaced by Lizzie's own jarring voice as she finishes reciting the poem in a flat, uncomprehending monotone.

Things are not what they seem in art, and the increasingly idealized image of Lizzie that Rossetti has created in his art belies the increasingly wretched woman who turns to laudanum to escape the loneliness imposed on her by her husband's infidelity and self-indulgence. She finally makes her ultimate escape by taking a fatal overdose of the drug.

Rossetti's gradual physical decay is but a reflection of the moral decay that has come in the wake of his dissolute life. His corruption is clearly complete when he desecrates his wife's grave to retrieve the book of poems, which he had buried with her in a melodramatic gesture of compunction, in order to sell them. The shot of a hand reaching into the exhumed coffin to snatch the moldy volume from beside the decomposing corpse is one of the most grisly images that Russell has ever conjured up—but no more shocking than Rossetti's own behavior. Consequently the viewer does not muster much pity for Rossetti as he watches the broken old man gradually succumb to chloral addiction.

In the last scene the desiccated Rossetti laboriously climbs once more to the top of a hillside overlooking a lake. We have seen him there earlier in the springtime of his youth with Lizzie when the trees were lush in their foliage. Now, in the gloomy autumn of his life, the scene has turned appropriately bleak, epitomized by a single gnarled and leafless tree near which he stands to contemplate his wasted life and lost loves. Then he begins his disconsolate descent down the hillside and disappears from sight as the film draws to a close.

Russell lightens the tone of this dark film from time to time by introducing cheerful popular songs on the sound track during the film and throughout the end credits. Nevertheless, these songs, anachronistic though they may be, are always appropriate to the story and to the theme of the movie. A steam calliope plays two numbers during the end credits: "If I Had a Talking Picture of You" to recall how Rossetti idealized Lizzie in his paintings and then was disappointed that the real girl could not match his glamorized artistic conception of her; and "I Want to Be Happy," a song which insists that one can only achieve joy by communicating it to others—a lesson which Rossetti learned too late in life, if at all.

Dante's Inferno ran a full ninety minutes and was the most difficult telefilm that Russell had directed up to that time. The cameraman was slow in lighting the scenes, and this irritated Oliver Reed and the other actors. The camera malfunctioned during the first week of shooting, moreover, and several scenes had to be done over. Furthermore, Russell had thought that he had made a virtue of necessity by hiring several amateur actors for minor roles, not only to help the budget but because these individuals really looked like the historical figures that they were portraying. But he soon discovered that, regardless of their physical resemblances to the characters they were enacting, several of them simply could not act—with the result that he had to curtail some of their performances severely in the final editing of the film.

Despite all of these technical and artistic difficulties, however, *Dante's Inferno* turned out to be a stunning film. After seeing it, Bryan Forbes, the feature director who had brought the original screenplay to Russell's attention, admitted to Russell that he regretted not having made the film himself.

Song of Summer: Frederick Delius 1968

Russell's next biopic is generally acknowledged, along with *Isadora*, to represent his finest work for television and to be among his best work in any medium. It concerns the British composer Frederick Delius (Max Adrian), who spent the last years of his life blind and crippled with syphilis, living in a French village with his wife, Jelka (Maureen Pryor), and his amanuensis Eric Fenby (Christopher Gable).

"It was a difficult TV film to make since I felt that I didn't know enough about Delius and his milieu," says Russell, "so I couldn't formulate just how I wanted to approach the material. But I went ahead with the Delius film anyhow since making films is always a voyage of discovery."

Dick Bush, who photographed *Delius* and several other Russell TV and feature films, agrees with Russell that shooting for TV does not differ essentially from shooting a theatrical film. "Some directors don't think that you can use long shots with a lot of extras filling the screen in a TV film," Bush remarks. "But I believe that such sequences can work on the small screen just as well as on the big screen. After all, theatrical features which were not originally shot with TV primarily in mind still look good on the small screen, even if they have a lot of long shots with detailed visual composition. The detail and care that you put into a scene pay off; even if the TV audience doesn't notice it consciously it will affect them subconsciously. A film made for television doesn't have to be an endless succession of close-ups."

Song of Summer is not so much about the dying Delius as it is about Eric Fenby, who had to face the frustration of subordinating his own career as a composer to that of a man who was making, he decided, a greater contribution to Britain's musical heritage than he ever would. Russell had initially tried to tell Delius's story by focusing on the composer primarily, rather than on his amanuensis; but that approach to the material, he discovered, yielded little dramatic conflict and did little to illuminate the inner man or his work. But after reading Fenby's biography of Delius, he realized that the story of Delius and Fenby represented one personality being fed on by another, one person saving another and being destroyed for his trouble.

"It's the most Catholic film I have ever done," Russell comments; "Fenby was a newly converted Catholic when he volunteered to help Delius; and he sacrificed himself, his life, and his future for an ideal and for a talent he thought greater than his own. Sacrifice is the central pivot of the Catholic Faith and one of the best things about it." *Song of Summer*, then, is the tale of how the man who sacrificed himself for another forever after feels that he was robbed of his own personal artistic vision. And the final irony, Russell concludes, is that a lot of Delius's music, "though it has moments of great beauty, is second-rate."[2]

Song of Summer and *Isadora* are two of Russell's most authentic biopics because in both cases he was able to collaborate with someone who had known the subject of each of the films personally in their last years. He was therefore able to get firsthand a great deal of the material which he needed for his film in each case.

During Russell's sessions with Fenby the latter would recreate incidents in his life with Delius in an extraordinarily genuine fashion by actually assuming the roles of both the aging composer and of the young disciple, and dramatizing their interaction for Russell. While he was working on the script, Russell would ask Fenby from time to time to recall a particular interchange between himself and the master, and Fenby would oblige by immediately repeating almost verbatim the substance of a given conversation.

Fenby was reluctant to allow Russell to reveal that Delius suffered and died from syphilis, since it was not generally known at the time and he had not even mentioned it in his 1936 biography of Delius. But Russell prevailed upon Fenby to let him include this fact in his script because Delius had, after all, been dead thirty years, and because Fenby finally accepted Russell's "warts and all" concept of biographical films.

Moreover, presenting an unvarnished portrait of Delius was really in total harmony with Fenby's own remark in his book on Delius that although commentators on the life of an artist should applaud the creator for developing his powers with diligence, "let them not make a god of him, for these creators are apt to turn out, after all, to be mere men, with the failings of men, like the rest of us," Fenby wrote. "The musician Delius was greater than the man. He lives for us now in his music, and not by reason of his outstanding qualities as a man."[3] And of course Fenby put up with the heartless behavior of Delius the man because of his abiding respect for Delius the composer.

The tone of Fenby's subservient relationship with Delius is subtly foreshadowed in the opening sequence of the film in which Fenby is discovered thumping out background music on an organ for a silent Laurel and Hardy comedy in a 1920s movie house. He is already accustomed, one infers, to subordinating his musical talent to external forces, as in this case, in which he is pictured adjusting his musical inspiration to the dictates of the silent comedy for which he is providing accompaniment.

Later, at the composer's home in France, Fenby is to be still more stifled by the suffocating atmosphere of the constricted world which the invalid Delius forces him to share. Delius may be immobilized physically, but his domineering personality gradually paralyzes Fenby psychologically. This point is underscored by the brief visit of Delius's friend and fellow composer Percy Grainger (David Collings). Fenby's loss of physical vitality, suggested by his failure to keep up with Grainger in jogging down a country lane, implies that a more severe psychic exhaustion has also overtaken Fenby during his term of confinement in Delius's remote country cottage. The cottage, in turn, symbolizes the insulated, egocentric world which the possessive and overbearing composer inhabits, and which he has imposed on both his wife and his amanuensis.

Delius's myopic selfishness, which renders him oblivious to the insensitive way in which he treats others, is brilliantly illustrated in the pair of flashbacks in which first he, then Grainger and Jelka, recall for Eric how they carried the invalid up a mountainside in a sedan chair to view one last sunset before his eyesight totally vanished. When shown from Delius's point of view, the little caravan is seen at a distance gliding smoothly up a mountain path in bright sunlight. When shown from the point of view of Grainger and Jelka, however, the friend and wife are pictured in close-up, sweating and straining with their burden, stumbling along a rocky road in a bleak fog. Delius, it seems, at times has taken advantage of Grainger as well as of his wife and of Eric; but always he remains unaware of the weight of the demands which he makes on others.

Still, all of them are as enamored of Delius's music as the composer himself is. When Jelka puts on an old 78 RPM record of one of Delius's compositions, the scratchy surface noise melts away as we hear on the sound track the way that the swelling chords become vividly alive in the minds and imaginations of the transfixed listeners. Such scenes imply

Song of Summer: (top) Ken Russell directing Max Adrian as the composer
Frederick Delius with David Collings as Percy Grainger; (bottom) Christopher Gable (Eric Fenby) and Maureen Pryor (Jelka Delius) at the bier of the
composer (credits: BBC-TV).

that Delius the composer does in fact transcend the shortcom-
ings of Delius the man; and this thought is nowhere more ef-
fectively conveyed than in the final scene of the film.

As Fenby and Jelka sprinkle the deceased Delius with rose
petals, the BBC follows its announcement of his death with a
moment from the composer's Song of Summer. Both Delius's
amanuensis and his widow weep softly, realizing that the balm
of the composer's music will somehow serve to soothe the
psychic wounds which they have suffered from the selfish and
manipulative human being; for he is gone from their lives but
his music remains.

Fenby later approved Russell's film wholeheartedly, declar-
ing it to be "Delius exactly as I remembered him." In fact, the
film was so true to life that Fenby wept uncontrollably the day
that he watched the shooting. And shortly after the film was
telecast he suffered a nervous collapse similar to the one
which he had experienced after parting with Delius temporar-
ily in 1933. The film had revived his deep-seated emotional
conflict about what subordinating his musical career to Delius's had done to his professional life, a conflict which Russell had made the center of the film.

Some Delius fans were unhappy that Russell had depicted
the underside of the composer's character in the film, but their
criticism was nothing compared to the protests that greeted
Russell's last biopic for the BBC.

The Dance of the Seven Veils: Richard Strauss (1970)

The complete title of Russell's film on Strauss, telecast on
February 15, 1970, was *The Dance of the Seven Veils: A Comic
Strip in Seven Episodes on the Life of Richard Strauss*. But the
musical establishment, not to mention the late Strauss's family
and publishers, were not amused by Russell's severe if
humorous caricature of Strauss. Nonetheless Russell remains
convinced that he had to make the film in the manner in which
he did.

"In every film I have made, the style has been dictated by
the subject. *Delius* was an austere, restrained film, mainly
about three people in a bare, white sick room. That was the
way to do that particular story. Strauss, on the other hand, was
a self-advertising, vulgar, commercial man. I took the keynote

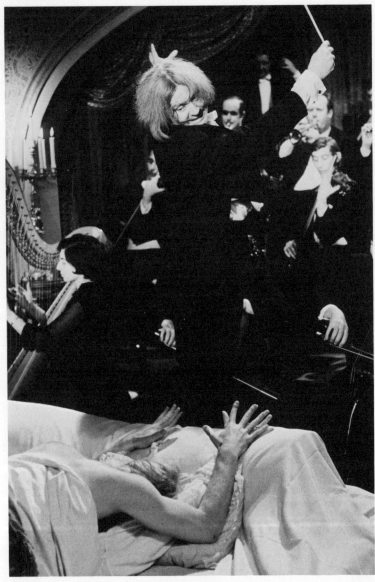

Ken Russell conducts the orchestra in *The Dance of the Seven Veils*
(credit: BBC-TV).

of the film from his music, a lot of which is bombastic and includes such egotistical items as an hour-long symphony about himself entitled A Hero's Life; then there is the Domestic Symphony, which requires an enlarged symphony orchestra to recreate a day in the Strauss household. I built up my portrait from the man himself; 95 percent of what Strauss says in the film he actually did say in his letters and other writings—which is why I gave him a screen credit for contributing to the dialogue."

In addition to giving Strauss the treatment he thought Strauss deserved, Russell in this film was out to make again a point about the nature of filmed biographies which he had made before. "I saw that television biographies were becoming filled with terrible clichés that had grown out of imitation of my earlier TV films: deification of the artist is wrong; he should be presented as a human being who, despite his faults, managed to create lasting works of art. Besides, the telecast began with an announcement that what was to follow was a harsh and violent personal interpretation of Strauss's life and work, but one which was nevertheless based on real events. This should have been a sufficient warning to those who might be offended by watching it."

Russell lampoons Strauss's foisting his private life on the concert public in his Domestic Symphony by picturing himself conducting the work in the Strauss bedroom while Mr. and Mrs. Strauss make love. The conductor accommodates the orchestra's performance of the piece to the rhythm of Strauss's performance on the bed, so that Strauss and the orchestra reach a climax simultaneously.

Still Russell feels that those who were offended by the film took it much too literally and therefore failed to realize that it was working on a deeper level than just satire. "For example," Russell points out, "in order to get across the fact that Richard Strauss was uninterested in the First World War because it didn't touch him personally, I presented a dream sequence in which Strauss (Christopher Gable) is forced to watch his wife raped and his child murdered by the enemy. Just as an enemy soldier holds a gun to Strauss's head, the image dissolves into that of his son with a toy gun, and then the camera pulls back to show the Strauss family in a kind of *Sound of Music* Tyrolean setting which is completely removed from the realities of the war. This is the insulated atmosphere in which Strauss wrote his Alpine Symphony—as if the war wasn't going on."

Russell scores the point about Strauss's indifference to the atrocities of the war again later in the film during a scene in which Strauss is conducting his Rosenkavalier waltzes while SS men torture a Jew in the concert audience by carving a Star of David on his chest with a knife. Strauss deigns to notice this intrusion on his lush romantic music only to the extent of signaling the orchestra to play louder in order to drown out the Jew's screams.

The symbolic intent of the film is further illustrated in the way that Russell portrays Strauss's relationship to the Nazi regime. Strauss thought of himself as an ageless superman, Russell notes; Strauss based his Zarathustra tone poem (which has since become identified with Kubrick's use of it in 2001) on Nietzsche's concept of the superman. Then in later years, when he was out of favor with Hitler, Strauss wrote an obsequious letter to him. "At this point," as Russell describes it, "I have his wife put on Strauss the mask of an old man, for Strauss has finally admitted his weakness and dependence on Hitler's favor. Later, after the war, when he is conducting the Zarathustra in London after he has been completely exonerated by the allies of having endorsed the Nazi regime, the music swells to a crescendo and I have Strauss rip off the mask of the old man: he is still the crypto-Nazi with the superman complex underneath the façade of the distinguished elderly composer."

The day following the telecast a motion was introduced in Parliament condemning Russell's version of Strauss's life and music as vicious, savage, and brutal. Some television critics suggested that he was trying to increase the limits of what is permissible on television. "The BBC did get an enormous number of phone calls after the film was televised, but as many for as against," Russell counters. "The members of the television audience are all asleep in their armchairs. It's a good thing to shake them up; even if it's only as far as the telephone. Huw Wheldon, then managing director of BBC-TV, defended the film when it was shown for fifty members of Parliament; and John Trevelyan, the British film censor at the time, supported the film as well."

Dance of the Seven Veils remains one of the most visually imaginative pieces of work that Russell ever did for the small screen, particularly in the fantasy sequences, whose comic-strip quality is highlighted by the garish color scheme of this, Russell's only color film for the BBC. John Baxter summed up the film best in his book on Russell when he wrote that it is a movie that is as much ballet as documentary, rich in images of lyric and occasionally demonic fantasy, all accompanied by Strauss's thundering music on the sound track.

In one scene, for instance, Russell brings Strauss's Don Juan tone poem to life by picturing Strauss, who styles himself in his voice-over commentary as a lady's man like Don Juan, wearing Erich Von Stroheim's white officer's uniform and monocle from *Foolish Wives* as he seduces a woman on the floor of her opera box while her husband is busy ogling the voluptuous diva onstage. When her husband at last notices what is going on, he and Strauss fight a duel that winds up with them capering through the orchestra pit like the Marx Brothers in the finale of *A Night at the Opera*.

Russell's burlesque of Strauss and his music carries right into the end credits of the film, during which an old Gershwin song called "A Melody by Strauss," which Russell borrowed from *An American in Paris*, is sung on the sound track (the song actually refers to Johann Strauss, but no matter). As Russell's own screen credit as director appears on the screen, he again is seen, in an inset above his name, as the wirey-haired conductor flailing away at leading the orchestra in Strauss's Domestic Symphony. Then he turns, bows, and leaves the podium. That last image of Russell was in point of fact a prophetic one, for after *Dance of the Seven Veils* Russell bowed out of the BBC for good.

After the BBC sought to mollify critics of the film (including Strauss's family and publisher) by presenting a roundtable discussion in which conductors and music pundits denounced Russell and his film, Russell decided to part company with the network once and for all. In the more than ten years that he had been associated with the BBC he had made three theatrical features, the third of which, *Women in Love* in 1969, had made a name for him in movie circles in much the same way that *Elgar* had made a name for him in TV circles a few years

earlier. Because *Women in Love* had now opened doors for
him in the film industry, Russell thought it an appropriate
time to pursue a career in feature films.

But Russell did not leave the television industry without regrets. The great thing about television, he feels, is that one can
make and screen a controversial film before anyone has had
time to place obstacles in the way; whereas the planning of a
motion picture moves much more slowly, so that, in the case of
the Strauss film, any number of people could have inhibited
the making of the film before it ever got into production as a
feature.

Nevertheless, the price which one pays with a really controversial TV film, Russell adds, is that it is suppressed and
rarely if ever shown again. "If I could feel that the films that I
did for television were shown all over the world at frequent
intervals," he concludes, "I'd probably never make a so-called
feature film again."[4] After making a string of feature films between 1970 and 1977, Russell did return to television to make
two other biopics, but this time for Granada-TV, an independent network, not for the BBC.

Clouds of Glory: Wordsworth and Coleridge (1978)

As early as the fall of 1972 Russell revealed in a letter his
desire "to return to the small screen of TV and get back to a
more personal and optimistic kind of film—something simple
that doesn't involve eighty people and where you wind up
with MGM." In the spring of 1975, when Russell was casting
about for a property to follow *Lisztomania* on his production
schedule, he mentioned in another letter several of the projects that had been offered him and concluded, "I keep promising myself to sit in a rocking chair in the Lake District and
make 16mm television specials on Wordsworth and the other
Lake poets; so maybe I will."

Then, in the summer of 1977 he wrote from the Lake District that he was busy preparing to shoot three one-hour telefilms about the Lake Poets with the overall title of *Clouds of
Glory*: "Yes my dream has come true at last; after talking about
it for years, to the BBC among others. Granada-TV got to hear
about it through one of their producers, none other than Norman Swallow, who was instrumental in getting me into the

BBC. Well, now he's done it again, but this time for the BBC's rivals. Writing the scripts is Melvyn Bragg," who had scripted *The Debussy Film*, *The Music Lovers*, and other Russell TV and feature films. "The BBC plans a year ahead and is pretty inflexible. Norman knew this and promised me that if the project was approved I could start filming in September, which is fine; whereas planning one's life twelve months ahead is not. Granada gave me their decision that they could afford to do the Lake Poets project in eight days, which is pretty astounding. David Hemmings is Samuel Taylor Coleridge, David Warner is William Wordsworth, and Felicity Kendal is Dorothy Wordsworth.

"The first film is the love story of William and Dorothy Wordsworth; the second features Samuel Taylor Coleridge and Thomas De Quincey, and deals with their addiction to the Lakes as well as to opium; the third film is 'King of the Crocodiles,' about the minor poet Robert Southey who nevertheless played a big part in the lives of the others. The central characters appear in each of the films since they were all inextricably mixed together—in more ways than one. Dick Bush, who photographed *Isadora*, *Delius*, *Mahler*, *Savage Messiah*, and *Tommy*, is the cameraman, and Shirley is doing the costumes. We are all thrilled about it."[5]

Punch playfully satirized Russell's biopics by publishing in its October 19, 1977, issue a parody which speculated on what a film by Ken Russell about Wordsworth might be like. Wordsworth would be, *Punch* conjectured, a poet and man of action who "hacked, raped, and pillaged his way through the French Revolution," and, when Paris became too hot for him, went into hiding in the Lake District of England, where the hills soon rang "with the screams of terrified country girls and sheep." Needless to say, *Clouds of Glory* turned out to be quite different from what the *Punch* satirist had imagined. But to some extent it also turned out somewhat differently than Russell himself had anticipated.

For one thing, he decided to do two segments rather than three, and eliminated the Southey section. In working on *Clouds* from the earliest planning stages onward Russell learned that television production had gotten much more complex and costly than it was in the days when he was at the BBC, and hence he realized from the start that he could realistically do only a two-part film.

Clouds of Glory: (top) Ken Russell directing Felicity Kendal and David
Warner; (bottom), Kendal and Warner as Dorothy and William Wordsworth.

Clouds of Glory: (top) David Warner as Wordsworth; (bottom) David Hemmings as Samuel Taylor Coleridge (credits: BBC-TV).

"The *Strauss* film was the most ambitious telefilm that I did
in my BBC period," he explains, "and the crew only num-
bered two dozen people; whereas by the time I did *Clouds* the
unions dictated that I use twice that number. I had to have two
continuity girls instead of one, and each of them had to have
an assistant! And there were no less than six prop men: two to
fetch the props, two to arrange them on the set, and two to take
them away at the end of shooting. The budget, therefore, was
much bigger than I had expected it to be, and Granada asked
me to economize further; so I decided not to employ any grips
to move the camera since I either had to have two or none at
all. As a result *Clouds* is the first film I have done for twenty
years in which there are virtually no tracking shots. Yet the
film does not look static since the camera still pans and tilts
throughout. I have discovered that there is something to be
said for this sort of simplicity. Perhaps I have used too much
camera movement in the past. In any case, many of the scenes
are set in small country cottages that did not allow for much
camera movement anyway."

Clouds of Glory was shot for the most part in the area
around Russell's work cottage in the Lake District, terrain that
will be familiar to those who have seen some of his earlier
telefilms such as *Rossetti* and *Delius*, as well as features like
Tommy and *The Devils*. Since Wordsworth and Coleridge actually lived there, however, the location is more appropriate
for *Clouds* than for any other Russell film.

In "William and Dorothy," the first segment, Wordsworth
and his sister range through the countryside together from
childhood onward. Neither seems to be aware that their in-
separable relationship is creating an emotional attachment
that will be hard to alter when either of them contemplates
marriage in the years ahead. In fact William, who is the more
emotionally stable of the pair, assures his sister that their bond
will always remain unimpaired even if one of them does
marry. Dorothy seems tentatively reassured–until she reads
one of Wordsworth's poems about the peasant girl Lucy, "She
Dwelt among the Untrodden Ways," in which Lucy dies. "I
am Lucy and you have killed her," Dorothy cries hysterically;
"your poem tells me that in your soul you have buried our
love."

Years later, as Dorothy lies ill and close to death, she recalls this incident, as well as others from her past life with William which are presented to the viewer in the form of flashbacks. Standing by her bedside is Mary Wordsworth, the woman William did eventually marry. Dorothy notices Mary's wedding ring and remembers the ominous day of Mary's marriage to William. In flashback we see William coming to his sister's room and begging her to come to the wedding. She refuses, but instead removes her dead mother's wedding ring from her finger and tells William to give it to Mary during the ceremony "with her blessing."

William momentarily slips the ring back on Dorothy's finger, kisses her hand, and then removes it for good. Shortly it will grace the hand of his new wife. William's gesture obviously symbolizes that he and his sister will remain linked by the same ring that he is giving to his bride; but the inconsolable Dorothy mutters, "We will never be alone again."

What Dorothy fails to realize is that she will be as much of an intrusion in Mary's relationship with William as Mary is in her relationship with William; and this Russell suggests in the very next scene. When the bride and groom return from the wedding, Dorothy stands in the cottage door to greet them, then promptly passes out. In his consternation William rushes to pick up his prostrate sister and carries her into the house—unaware that he has left his bride, whom he should have carried over the threshold, standing alone in the dusty road.

Dorothy never fully reconciles herself to losing William, and hence all of her repressed emotions surface as she lies fevered and delirious in what she assumes is her final illness. Meanwhile William roams the countryside waiting for the end and meets an admirer of his work who suggests that one of William's own poems should offer him consolation in the event of his sister's death:

> Not in entire forgetfulness,
> And not in utter nakedness,
> But trailing clouds of glory do we come
> From God who is our home.

William returns home and finds Dorothy smiling down at him from her bedroom window. The end has been delayed, but for how long?

" 'William and Dorothy' is the most subdued film I have
done since *Delius* and *Savage Messiah*," says Russell; and he
is quite right. William and Dorothy's unresolved emotional
conflict is beautifully understated in the film, and yet it is always there, simmering just beneath the surface of the conventional lives which they lead. Theirs was a love that dare not
speak its name, and since neither of them ever explicitly
verbalized the incestuous dimension of their relationship, that
dimension is implied but never stated in so many words anywhere in the film. Standard accounts of Wordsworth's life
bear out the facts of the case as Russell has depicted them in
the movie, and indicate that he has not overstated them in his
dramatization of William and Dorothy's lives.

No one could exaggerate the facts of Coleridge's lurid life,
which allows Russell a free reign in the use of fantasy as well
as flashbacks to portray his tragic and wild experiences. Russell entitled this second part of *Clouds of Glory* "The Rime of
the Ancient Mariner" after Coleridge's celebrated poem of
that title because, as he points out, "Coleridge himself said
that he *was* the ancient mariner. So I thought of seeing his
whole life in terms of that poem. I had always thought about
the albatross which the mariner kills as being a metaphor for
Coleridge's subconscious wish to be rid of his estranged wife,
and when I reread the poem it seemed to fit; and so I presented it that way in the film."

The format of "The Rime of the Ancient Mariner" consists
of Coleridge's reciting lines from the poem over the sound
track while various scenes from his real life and his fantasy life
are portrayed on the screen. Reality and fantasy blend into
each other in the course of the film since they did so in the life
of Coleridge the opium addict, who could not always distinguish clearly between the two.

The opening sequence of the Coleridge film clearly establishes Russell's deft intermingling of illusion and reality. Coleridge rummages madly through his study in a futile search for
a bottle of laudanum, hurtling books and manuscripts to the
floor and smashing furniture. As the opening lines of "The
Rime" are heard voice-over, reality gives way to illusion: in
the ensuing fantasy sequence Coleridge drifts aimlessly in a
boat until his wife suddenly materializes before him and he
brutally buries the anchor in her breast, since she represents
to him the albatross that is blighting his existence.

"It is a sequence of such power and ferocity, of such majesty and sustained definance," wrote Tony Palmer in the Sunday *Telegraph*, "that in my opinion it dwarfs almost everything else seen on television in the last decade." Never again, he continued, will we be able to think of the music of Ralph Vaughan Williams, which is used in the Coleridge film, "as only a dream of the English countryside; never again will we be able to read of the Ancient Mariner and tell our children that English poetry is nice and harmless." Russell, Palmer concluded, has once again proved that "he is just the best English film director we have."[6]

The interplay of fantasy and reality in Coleridge's life is also well illustrated in the scene in which he contemplates suicide. Russell intercuts shots of Coleridge brandishing the knife with which he means to stab himself with shots of the symbolic figures of Death and Life from the "Mariner" poem casting lots to determine whether Coleridge should live or die. Just as the dice roll in favor of Life, Coleridge drops the knife and determines to go on living.

Russell has never been at a loss for visual metaphors, and there is one in particular that pervades "Mariner" that is well worth mentioning. He implies that Coleridge's drug addiction has caused him to regress into irresponsible, infantile behavior by associating Coleridge several times in the course of the film with children. When Coleridge is in the throes of his craving for opium his wife cradles him in her arms like a little child; late in the film, when he is undergoing treatment to control his addiction, the wife of his sympathetic doctor spoon-feeds him his daily ration of opium as if he were a little boy taking medicine.

Coleridge in the end does gain some degree of maturity and peace of mind, and offers a prayer from the "Mariner" poem which closes the second part of *Clouds*, and which represents a tremendous Amen to life that seems to serve as a touching epilogue for the whole of *Clouds of Glory*:

> He prayeth best who loveth best
> All things both great and small;
> For the dear God who loveth us
> He made and loveth all.

Although "William and Dorothy" and "The Rime of the Ancient Mariner" have some degree of narrative continuity

(William and Dorothy appear in the Coleridge episode, for example), they in many ways are two very different films. Russell's directorial style is more subtle and controlled in the Wordsworth segment because the dramatic conflict that lies at the heart of it is less close to the surface than in the Coleridge story, in which the dramatic conflict is more overt. Hence the two parts of *Clouds* complement each other nicely, and together make up a film whose two sections are integrated into a satisfying whole, while at the same time each of the two parts retains its individuality as a separate episode that is complete in itself. Consequently, although the two one-hour episodes were premiered on successive Sunday evenings in the summer of 1978 on British television, they could easily be shown together on the same evening, since the viewer's appreciation of each is enhanced by seeing both.

With his return to TV biopics seven years after he had left the BBC to devote himself to feature films, Russell's career has come full circle. "TV production has grown more complex and expensive over the years, as I discovered while making *Clouds of Glory*," he says; "but even so I couldn't have made *Clouds* for anything like the same budget if it had been a feature film." One suspects that Russell's future career may include work in both media since he has firmly established himself in both. Yet, as we shall shortly see, Russell's two initial ventures in the cinema were so unpromising that it seemed for a time that he might never succeed as a feature director.

3

The Mature Movie Maker: The Early Feature Films

BECAUSE OF the consistent interest that Russell's television documentaries had occasioned by 1963, he was invited by British producer Ken Harper to venture into the world of cinema. Although the project was not one that he would have chosen himself, Russell thought he should take advantage of the opportunity to make his mark in the movie industry.

French Dressing (1963)

Russell remembers *French Dressing* as "a kind of seaside comedy which was an ill-conceived project from the start: the chemistry of the characters was wrong and the story never quite jelled." Yet he began the project with enthusiasm; he saw it not only as his door into feature films but also as a release from making biopics, since he feared going stale if he continued working in that genre indefinitely. Also the script was being written by two writers known for their flair for comedy, Peter Meyers and Ronald Cass.

Russell and the writing team scouted locations for the settings of the film, which was to be about a tawdry English resort town that tries to attract a wider clientele by inaugurating both an international film festival and a nudist beach in the same summer season. The trio holed up in a dilapidated hotel at Herne Bay and began knocking out a script which Russell found forced and artificial. So he convinced Harper to bring in Peter Brett, the actor who had played Elgar as a young man and who was also a promising writer. The screenplay grew to no less than 200 pages with nary a funny line anywhere in sight. Still, Russell thought, the situations were humorous and would make a farcical film, especially since the stars were to

75

Glenda Jackson and Oliver Reed in the film version of D. H. Lawrence's Women in Love *(credit: United Artists)*.

be James Booth and Roy Kinnear, both of whom had proven comic abilities.

But Russell had not yet reckoned with the fact that he had never before directed professional actors to any great degree, since his BBC films up to that time had depended more on artful camera set-ups and picturesque landscapes than on the performances of the actors, who spoke no dialogue and only pantomimed their roles. He therefore felt inexperienced and ill at ease in directing professionals of the caliber of Booth and Kinnear when shooting began; and they sensed his feelings when they observed him spending more time working out the lighting and visual composition of a scene than he did in coaching them in their parts.

Little wonder that one newspaper account of the production described Russell's pensive and preoccupied manner on location as that of a monklike man in communion with himself, converting the space immediately around him into an intangible cloister.

The storyline of the movie never developed beyond the level of insipid farce. Jim, the hero (James Booth), and his sidekick, Henry (Roy Kinnear), find their plans going very much awry: the film festival collapses in a riot on opening night and Françoise Fayol, the French sex symbol (Marisa Mell) whom they have engaged to preside over the festivities, reneges on taking part in the opening of the nudist beach. Jim's own girl friend, Judy (Alita Naughton), fills in for her in the middle of a cloudburst. By this point even Jim is thoroughly ashamed of himself and his finagling; at the cliché-ridden finale Jim, Judy, and Henry set out all smiles to start life anew.

Nevertheless the finished film has some interesting directorial bits that presage better Russell movies to come. When Françoise, the bargain-basement Brigitte Bardot, arrives in town, the mayor honors her with a parade. Before he and Françoise realize what is happening, the reviewing stand, which happens to be on the back of a truck, rolls down a ramp and into the sea while "Brittania Rules the Waves" is solemnly intoned on the sound track by a massive choir.

During the opening-night premiere of Françoise's new film, a brawl breaks out in the auditorium in the middle of the screening. Jim is hurled through the movie screen just as a close-up appears of Françoise with her mouth open wide, so that the impression is that she has swallowed him alive. Then Russell cuts to the real Françoise with mouth agape in a scream of despair as the riot continues all around her. But these interesting touches were not enough to save the film from oblivion.

The reception after the press screening, which Russell made the mistake of attending, was like a wake at which he was the corpse. He got drunk and vowed to go back to television and stay there. The reviews were uniformly negative, with one critic calling the film a mixture of slapstick and satire put together in a pretentious and undisciplined manner that demonstrated just how difficult it can be to capture good screen comedy on film. The picture opened with little publicity, was severely shortened to serve as a second feature on double bills, and disappeared altogether without receiving any release at all in the United States. Russell kept his resolution to stay with the BBC for the next four years, a peak period for his TV work in which he consistently turned out biopics of a high order, including *Debussy* and *Isadora*.

Billion Dollar Brain (1967)

Then, in 1967, Russell signed a contract with producer Harry Saltzman to film the life of the Russian dancer Vaslav Nijinsky, but the project was shelved when Rudolf Nureyev lost interest in it. "He decided that he could not play the role of a dancer inferior to himself," said Russell sardonically at the time. As a warm-up for this biopic which ultimately never happened, Russell directed the spy film *Billion Dollar Brain* for Saltzman instead, with Michael Caine playing the secret agent Harry Palmer, whom Saltzman hoped would inspire a cult similar to that of the James Bond films, with which he was also associated. But by this time moviegoers had had their fill of the glut of spy films on the market, so *Billion Dollar Brain* did not catch on.

Another problem with the movie was its hopelessly complicated plot, based on Len Deighton's slick novel of the same name, in which Palmer collaborates with the Russian Colonel Stok (Oscar Homolka) to overturn a plot hatched by General Midwinter, a mad Texas millionaire (Ed Begley), to foment

Michael Caine, Françoise Dorleac and Karl Malden in *Billion Dollar Brain* (1967) (credit: Movie Star News).

war between Russia and the United States by meddling in the internal politics of Latvia. Given the fact that Midwinter has his own private army of mercenaries, and monitors world affairs with the aid of a huge computer complex (the billion dollar brain), he is no mean adversary.

Russell and screen writer John McGrath eventually gave up trying to whip the story into shape and concentrated on creating some visually exciting sequences which admittedly had little to do with the plot line. The most spectacular of these set pieces serves as the climax of the film and involves the disappearance of Midwinter's army beneath the icy waters of the Baltic Sea. This sequence was deliberately conceived by Russell as a homage to the battle on the ice in Eisenstein's costume epic *Alexander Nevsky*, to which a passing reference is made in Deighton's novel. In the Eisenstein film (a clip from which Russell included in his BBC documentary on Prokofiev, who scored the film) the invading Teutonic knights are held back by the Russian army as they attempt to cross the frozen surface of Lake Peipus until finally the ice gives way. The enemy sinks beneath the crumbling ice into the freezing waters, as if the jaws of some chilly hell have opened to swallow them.

In Russell's version of this classic scene, Midwinter's army, complete with tanks and trucks, in substituted for the Teutonic knights; but the outcome of the battle is the same. Russell, who was to some extent still looked upon as an upstart fugitive from TV by the veteran members of the movie crew, wanted to shoot his battle on the ice on location, while his staff sided with the front office in maintaining that it could be accomplished by the use of the studio tank. Simulated ice was spread over the studio tank; but as the technical crew manipulated the model vehicles around its surface by remote control, Russell felt that the toy trucks and tanks which kept bumping into each other looked very phony indeed. He finally convinced the studio to let him shoot the scene out-of-doors, with real vehicles and freezing water, with the result that the whole scene was much more effective.

Another fine episode in the film is the precredit sequence, which unfortunately promised a better all-around spy movie than actually was delivered. A shadowy figure breaks into Harry's squalid combination office-flat and surveys the tell-

tale indications of Harry's failure as a private investigator: a
derelict shoe with a hole in the sole, a soiled sink overflowing
with unwashed dishes, a box of corn flakes stashed in a file
drawer where the dossiers of active cases ought to be. The
intruder turns out to be Harry's former boss in Her Majesty's
Secret Service, who is assuring himself that Harry is desperate
enough to be willing to return to work for the government.

This opening scene of the movie, in which an apparent foe
turns out to be a friend, sets the pattern for the balance of the
film, in which there is such a snarl of spies and counterspies,
agents and double agents, that Harry—and the audience—is
always at a loss to know for sure who is working with him and
who is working against him. This aspect of the plot does create
some notable moments of suspense and surprise.

Moreover, Russell implies that Harry is operating in an alien
and hostile environment where he can never feel more than
momentarily secure by several dandy visual images. Harry, for
example, arrives in Helsinki shivering in a London trenchcoat
completely unsuited to the severe Finnish winter. More than
once he is framed by bare, gnarled tree limbs silhouetted
against a bleak, wintry sky, symbolic of the chilly atmosphere
of icy foreboding in which he is moving.

Even the contrasting warm weather of General Midwinter's
ranch is no more reassuring, since Russell associates the Texas
heat with the fevered atmosphere which the obsessed General
Midwinter has created around him. Midwinter's madness is
further projected by the raging bonfire before which he stands
while delivering a fiery speech to his devoted followers to in-
flame still more their fascist feelings.

Though critics in general liked what they called the occasional extravagant touches in Russell's direction of *Billion
Dollar Brain*, the picture was a commercial failure, partially
because Russell had made the Russians, represented by Colonel Stok, look so good, and the Americans, represented by
General Midwinter, look so bad. In addition, the virtually in-
decipherable plot was an enormous drawback as well. *Time's*
review is typical of the movie's reception: "By the time that
Oscar Homolka, as the genial head of Russia's secret service,
stops Midwinter's army cold, viewers may decide that the
whole thing is mechanical enough to have been turned out by

a computer—and one that is worth a lot less than a billion dollars.''[1]

In retrospect Russell felt that the subject matter of the movie was simply too alien to him to allow him to do a creditable job of direction. "I didn't know what a Texas millionaire was like or an American fascist either, and Midwinter was both," he has since said. "I tried doing the film the best way I could, but I just couldn't believe in it. I'm really much more at home in the past."

So it was back to television for Russell, who then made two fine biopics on Rossetti and Delius. The success of these two films encouraged United Artists, who thought that Russell had been treated unfairly, in particular by right-wing reviewers of *Billion Dollar Brain*, to give him another chance.

Women in Love (1969)

He agreed to do a screen version of D. H. Lawrence's 1920 novel, *Women in Love*, the film that was to mark him at long last as a mature movie maker. Lawrence himself never had much respect for the cinema, and criticized the romantic and unrealistic way that the early films of his time often portrayed the love relationship in and out of marriage. In his view the only way that an individual could break out of his own sphere of isolation was to become totally involved with another human being in a love relationship which culminated in the sexual experience, but was not limited to it. His novel *Women in Love*, then, was basically about the pursuit for personal fulfillment in a love relationship, and about the sacrifices which one must make in achieving that fulfillment.

The two women of the title are sisters, Ursula and Gudrun. Gudrun is in love with the wealthy Gerald Crich and Ursula with his friend Rupert Birkin. Gerald becomes the pivotal character inasmuch as he cannot give himself totally to Gudrun in a love relationship any more than he can give himself to Birkin in a different way in friendship. Gerald consequently causes frustration and unhappiness all around, and finally takes his own life.

At the end of the novel Birkin tells Ursula, now his wife, that he has found fulfillment with her, but that he nonetheless regrets that Gerald was incapable of fulfilling him on the level of friendship. "You can't have two kinds of love," Ursula responds, "because it's false, impossible." "I don't believe that," he answers; nor, one infers, does Lawrence.

Lawrence wrote of human relations with a prose style filled with delicate nuances which are hard to translate onto film. But Russell was determined that his film would come as close to reflecting Lawrence's complex vision as possible. Hence he immersed himself completely in the novel before working on the script with Larry Kramer, who had already written a first draft in collaboration with another British director, Silvio Narrizano, for which Kramer and Narrizano were never able to find financing. Consequently, Kramer was eager to accept Russell as director if it meant getting the project off the shelf and into production.

Kramer was a competent screen writer, but Russell found the script a very poor approximation of the Lawrence book. "Kramer apparently believed," Russell remarks, "that unless a script writer changes his literary source beyond recognition, he is not being creative. As a result, this version of the screenplay had little to do with Lawrence. At the final fade-out Rupert and Ursula were to gallop off into the sunset. When I read that, I decided to take a hand in writing the script. I used as much of Lawrence's dialogue as I possibly could. Much of the conversation in the film is verbatim from the novel. For the story line, I pulled out of the novel's action the bits that would hang together as a narrative, and wrote transitional passages of dialogue to link these scenes together."

Russell would work on the script in the mornings and go to Kramer's flat in the afternoon and read him what he had written so far that day. Karmer would in turn type it up, making suggestions along the way. "Kramer wrote some good dialogue and we did retain two or three sequences from his original script," Russell concludes; "but I suppose that I am as responsible as anyone for the film's fidelity to Lawrence."

With the script well in hand, Russell took off on a tour of the countryside in search of location sites. The production staff on the film taught him to limit himself as much as possible to a twenty-five-mile radius in which to search for all of the locations which he would need, since less time spent in moving from one location to another would mean that more time could be devoted to actual shooting. With this in mind, Russell chose three centers which would encompass all of the needed locations.

Shooting commenced in September 1969 with the exterior sequences because Russell wanted to get them safely in the can before the unpredictable English winter weather began to set in. Although the actual time that Russell had to shoot the picture was limited, he had spent so much time preparing to direct the film beforehand that by the time shooting started he knew exactly what he wanted in each scene. He also found that the extensive experience which he had by now chalked up in TV was proving invaluable to him.

"Working in television, you learn how to cut costs and prune down a project to essentials," he says. "When you work fast you get a certain spontaneity from your cast and crew, and they make suggestions about how to improve a scene during shooting. I only work with people who understand what I am trying to do because of the short time we have to get the job done. In order to make a period picture on the same budget as a film in a contemporary setting you have to sacrifice something, and I sacrifice time. I assemble around me a cast and crew that can almost intuit what I want, and to whom, therefore, I have to say very little." Actors like Oliver Reed and Christopher Gable have worked for Russell several times and therefore are clearly Russell's kind of performers.

When Russell decided to include in the film the nude wrestling scene between Gerald (Oliver Reed) and Rupert (Alan Bates) which takes place in the novel, he discussed it with Reed and Bates. "I originally thought of a swimming context for the scene, since how else could you explain the two men stripping off for the match? Then Oliver Reed said that that kind of setting would be too poetic. He suggested instead that it should be more of a real physical confrontation between two men locked in a room sweating and straining; and that is how we finally did it."

At its conclusion Birkin says to Gerald, "We are mentally and spiritually close. Therefore we should be physically close too." "This is not a plea for a homosexual relationship," Russell explains. "Birkin is rather expressing to Gerald the same point of view about love relationships which he expresses to his wife at the end of the story. He believes that two men can

Oliver Reed and Alan Bates in the famed nude wrestling sequence from *Women in Love* (credit: United Artists).

each get married and yet maintain an intimate relationship with each other that is different from, but which nevertheless complements, the heterosexual relationship that each has in marriage. Gerald could not commit himself to Birkin on this level, not only because he thought such a relationship unconventional, but because he really could not reveal himself or commit himself to anyone."

It is significant that on the night on which Gerald decides to seduce Gudrun (Glenda Jackson) he is standing in front of the same fireplace before which he and Rupert wrestled; its blaze once again provides heat and light that seem not to penetrate his cold and gloomy exterior. The visual association which Russell wants to make here is that Gerald, having rejected Rupert's invitation to a close friendship, now decides to see if Gudrun can help him to overcome his inhibitions and to find in her the fulfillment which he craves.

Gudrun, however, is a strong-willed woman who will not allow herself to be dominated by any male, even one to whom she is attracted as much as she is to Gerald. Russell establishes this stubborn streak in Gudrun's personality in the scene in which Gudrun happens to witness Gerald's cruelly digging his spurs into the sides of his mare, urging it to gallop faster. Angry tears course down Gudrun's face as she senses the domineering, sadistic implications of Gerald's behavior; it is perhaps at this very moment that she resolves that Gerald will never master her as he has broken the spirit of his hapless mare.

Once their relationship has begun, Gerald chafes when he finds that Gudrun will not defer to his bidding in the way that everyone else seems to. "Try to love me a little more and want me a little less," she tells him. "You are crude; you break and waste me, and it is horrible to me." The crucial crisis in their deteriorating relationship arises on an Alpine vacation during which Gudrun taunts Gerald's masculinity by preferring to his company that of Loerke, a middle-aged homosexual (Vladek Sheybal). Gerald madly tries to choke the spirit out of Gudrun, whom he has not been otherwise able to subdue. It is the beginning of the end for Gerald, who then wanders off into the snowy wastes to die of exposure. At this point Russell rounds off the visual pattern of images of heat and cold that have been associated with Gerald throughout the film. Gerald would not

accept the human warmth offered him in different ways by
Gudrun and by Rupert, and symbolized by the flames of the
fireplace before which he contemplated both types of love.
His frigid personality, which is the underlying cause of his
ultimate rejection of a genuine love relationship of any kind, is
therefore reflected by the frosty slopes on which he finally
perishes. Gerald froze to death on the inside, from the
spiritual chill which permeated his existence, long before he
exposed himself to the Alpine winter.

Russell has neatly linked other patterns of visual images in
the film, a technique of his which is not only visually satisfying to the viewer but also helps him to grasp the continuity of
the multi-leveled plot. The film begins with the wedding of
Gerald's sister Laura to Tibby Lupton, and we see them em-
bracing for the first time on their wedding day; we see them
embrace for the last time as they lie intertwined in a deathly
clasp when their bodies are revealed in the receding waters of
the lake in which they have been drowned. This shot in turn
dissolves to one of Rupert and Ursula (Jennie Linden) in an
embrace that follows their having made love. The juxtaposi-
tion of these two contrasting images suggests that some relationships end prematurely in tragedy and death, as Tibby and
Laura's did, and as Gerald and Gudrun's will, whereas other
love relationships nurture happiness and life, as does Rupert
and Ursula's.

All the sumptuous visual imagery of the film helps to balance the sometimes heavy Lawrencian dialogue which can at
times be more difficult to comprehend when spoken from the
screen than when read on the page. The opening scene of the
film in the rough cut was an extended conversation between
Rupert and Ursula, in which Rupert as school inspector demonstrates to Ursula as a teacher in his charge how she might
best explain the facts of life to her students. In the course of
editing the film down to a little more than two hours, Russell
decided that this scene was too long and too ponderous for a
place so early in the movie, and would probably mean that he
would lose the audience's interest at the very outset of the
picture.

On the other hand, the scene established the professional
relationship of Rupert and Ursula, and implied that their ac-
quaintance would grow into something more intimate; so Rus-

sell could not simply remove it from the film altogether. After mulling over the problem for some days, he finally hit upon the perfect solution. He decided to intercut the scene as a flashback which Ursula recalls when she meets Rupert at Laura and Tibby's wedding. He accordingly extracted the essence of the schoolroom scene and interpolated it into the wedding scene as a flashback, and scrapped the rest of it.

The opening credits are superimposed on Ursula and Gudrun's trolley ride to the wedding. The musical background for this sequence is the Twenties tune "I'm Forever Blowing Bubbles," the lyrics of which suggest that both girls cherish unrealistic illusions about what it means to commit oneself to a love relationship, and that their immature notions about love and marriage are doomed to be burst like bubbles before they learn to love maturely.

By the end of the film the two women in love have learned what true love involves. Gudrun is forced to admit that two people cannot remain totally independent if they are to make the mutual compromises necessary for a successful union; and Ursula learns that even if one is prepared to make the compromises necessary to make a marriage work, no human relationship will ever be perfect, much less idyllic.

Women in Love proved to be Russell's biggest critical and popular success up to that point in his career. *Savage Messiah* was to find an equal number of admirers and *Tommy* would be an even bigger box-office triumph; but no other Russell film after *Women in Love* has pleased both the critics and the mass audience as much. Glenda Jackson won an Academy Award for her performance, and Larry Kramer, who received sole screen credit for the script, was nominated for an Oscar for the best screenplay of the year, while Russell himself was nominated as best director.

Russell was immediately offered the chance to translate several other important novels to the screen and toyed with the idea of doing movie versions of Graham Greene's *A Burnt-Out Case* and of Evelyn Waugh's 1934 novel *A Handful of Dust*. "If I were to do the Waugh film," Russell said at the time, "I would not attempt to update it to the present as the recent film of his 1928 novel *Decline and Fall* did. Waugh's novels are relevant to the present, and they do not have to have the setting updated to prove it."

Asked why he used so much of Lawrence's dialogue in the film of *Women in Love* when Graham Greene has said that when he adapts his own fiction to the screen he tends to write new dialogue for the script, Russell replied, "If one adapts one's own novel to another medium, he feels that he's done it this way once; in the interim it has grown in his mind, since one's ideas about any subject change and grow over a period of time. But if I adapt something written by someone else to the screen, I am approaching it fresh and want to leave the thing the way it was as much as possible."

Gradually Russell's thoughts began to turn away from doing another film adaptation of a major novel right away, since it would be hard to top *Women in Love*. Besides, one of the things which had captivated him about filming *Women in Love* in the first place, after doing so many television biopics, was that Lawrence had based his major characters on his own circle of friends. After the twin failure of *French Dressing* and *Billion Dollar Brain*, he reasoned that the only film projects that would be viable for him would be ones that were about real people or characters who were at least firmly anchored in reality. Rupert Birkin was a fictionalized portrait of Lawrence himself, for example, and Ursula was based to some degree on Lawrence's wife, Frieda. "This gave me a sort of factual foundation on which I could build a script," Russell says.[2]

It was not surprising, therefore, that his professed affinity for biographical subjects would lead him to choose to make a biopic for his next feature film. There was, in fact, a hint of what his next feature would be in *Women in Love*. In one scene Gudrun and Loerke, the homosexual she meets in the Alpine resort, parody the relationship of Tchaikovsky and his wife, Nina, referring to it as the marriage of "a homosexual composer and a scheming nymphomaniac." "That is a flip way of putting it," says Russell, "but basically that's what the story of Tchaikovsky's marriage boiled down to." And that is what became the subject of Russell's next film, *The Music Lovers*.

The film was to be financed by United Artists, whose confidence in Russell had been vindicated several times over by *Women in Love*. But this time Russell demanded and got the same artistic control of his new film that he had enjoyed at the BBC. "While I was at the BBC I was my own boss," Russell remarks. "And immediately after *Women in Love* I was ready to go back to television for good since I wasn't allowed to act as my own producer on that film or on either of my previous feature films. I found that when someone else is producing I have a battle royal with him most of the time. After one has poured his life blood into a project, it is difficult to accept the fact that someone else is really controlling it. But when United Artists finally offered me the same artistic freedom in making features that I had had in television, I decided to stick with motion pictures."

And so he did.

4

In Search of a Hero: The Biographical Feature Films

MORE THAN any other contemporary movie maker, Ken Russell has sought to liberate the biographical film from the clichés imposed upon it by the old-fashioned movie biographies of the past. "I love biographical period films," he explains. "The possibility of opening a book into the past fascinates me. You don't have to worry that every last detail is historically accurate; a lack of total authenticity doesn't matter; in the end a little roughness is not a bad thing. I generally select historical material because all of the stories I do are about the relationships of people to their environment and to each other, and about other eternal questions which we are just as concerned about today as people were in the past. Topics of the moment pass and change; besides, one's feelings towards contemporary topics tend to distort one's presentation of them. We can be much more dispassionate and objective, and therefore more truthful, in dealing with the past. To see things of the past from the vantage point of the present is to be able to judge what effect they have had on the present."

Russell's intent, then, is to give his audience some perspective on the present by seeing it in the context of the past. "Historical films are often made as if people living in the past thought of themselves as part of history already, living in museums," Russell continues. "But people in every century have thought of themselves as contemporary, just as we think of ourselves as contemporary."

Various interpreters of Russell's biopics have sought to define a thematic pattern in these films. Admittedly any such pattern would most likely have been developed subconsciously on Russell's part since creative intuition plays a role in the work of any serious artist. Nonetheless, such a pattern is

91

liver Reed as Father Grandier at the stake in The Devils *971) (credit: Warner Brothers)* .

well worth discerning if one is to see Russell's films as an expression of his personal vision.

Any Russell biopic presents the facts of a given subject's life in terms of Russell's own personal response to those historical facts; and it is from Russell's interpretation of the biographical facts of the historical figure's life that the theme of each biographical film emerges. In tracing the thematic development in these biographical films, I have found the theme which pervades Russell's biopics to be succinctly stated in the subtitle of Colin Wilson's 1974 monograph, *Ken Russell: A Director in Search of a Hero*.

Sophisticated modern directors like Bergman and Fellini have used their skills "to convey the message that life is tragic and futile," writes Wilson; "and here is Russell deliberately using the cinema to explore the view that man doesn't have to be defeated or destroyed." In his TV films on Delius, Rossetti, and Strauss, and in his feature film on Tchaikovsky, for example, he explored heroes who he felt had never realized their potential either as artists or human beings because they compromised their ideals in both their personal and professional lives. In *The Devils*, however, Russell's next feature after the Tchaikovsky film, he began to create his own blueprint for a genuine hero, Wilson maintains, a human being capable of transcending defeat and compromise. And, I might add, Wilson's insight also seems to apply to the heroes of Russell biopics made after Wilson's book appeared; for the heroes of *Savage Messiah* and of *Valentino* transcend defeat and compromise even more than the hero of *The Devils*.[1]

Even though it appeared before Wilson's monograph, Michael Dempsey's essay on Russell in *Film Quarterly* is useful in further fleshing out Wilson's theory about Russell's search for a hero in his biopics. Dempsey writes that Russell's central characters "seek to change, deny, or flee their identities." This is certainly true of Tchaikovsky in *The Music Lovers*, for instance: instead of trying to come to terms with his homosexuality, Tchaikovsky seeks to deny it by becoming entangled in a hopeless marriage.

But the individuals who fascinate the director most, Dempsey contends, are those who struggle against their own personalities, not to deny or obliterate any part of their self-identities, but "in order to achieve a level of existence that they regard as higher, more noble."² Father Grandier, the hero of *The Devils*, as we shall see, rightly tries to change from an ignoble and profligate priest to a true follower of his vocation, willing to sacrifice himself for others. So too later Russell heroes will, with varying degrees of success, endeavor to reconcile their talents with their personal aspirations in a meaningful way that will enable them to transcend their personal limitations and accomplish their goals. For me, Valentino, of all of Russell's heroes, will best embody Russell's concept of a hero as it has developed in his films, while Tchaikovsky most clearly falls beneath Russell's concept of a hero.

The Music Lovers (1970)

Russell became interested in Tchaikovsky when he heard the composer's First Piano Concerto for the first time on the radio, at the age of eighteen. He thought the second, slow movement of the concerto unbearably beautiful; and from that day to this has been a devoted music lover. Russell knew that sooner or later he would get around to doing a biopic about Tchaikovsky, but by the time he did so he had become disillusioned by learning about the tawdry life of a man whose music he had cherished since his teens.

Russell therefore was determined to dramatize what he saw as the enormous gap between Tchaikovsky's grimly unromantic life and his ravishingly romantic music. A Russian film on the life of Tchaikovsky was being made at the same time that Russell was preparing *The Music Lovers*, but he assured United Artists that his approach to the composer's life would be different from the Russian version. "For one thing, the Russians have never admitted that Tchaikovsky was homosexual," Russell notes. "Tchaikovsky himself said that his inner conflicts are there in his music, and so they are. His Sixth Symphony is tortured and tragic, since it expresses his frustrated and unhappy life, and he rightly entitled it *Pathetique* because his life was pathetic. In making *The Music Lovers* I followed the practice that I had established in my television biographies of great artists by making a definite connection between the man's life and his work. There is not one piece of Tchaikovsky's music that is used in the film that

is there for its own sake. It is all there to reflect some aspect of
Tchaikovsky's life and personality."

To play Tchaikovsky, Russell first chose Alan Bates of
Women in Love, but Bates declined; and in the end Russell
was pleased that he finally settled on Richard Chamberlain
because, quite simply, Chamberlain could not only play the
part but could play the piano as well. Were Chamberlain not at
least an amateur pianist, Russell would have had to use the
traditional dodge of Hollywood biographies about composers
of alternating close-ups of the face of the actor who is supposedly playing the piano with close-ups of someone else's
hands actually doing so. As it was, in the concert sequences
Russell could pan from the hands pounding away at the
keyboard up to the face of Chamberlain realistically miming
the performance of a Tchaikovsky work.

Chamberlain likewise fulfilled his acting chores conscienti-
ously, so much so that he later said that he had worked so hard
on *The Music Lovers* that after it was finished he was tempted
to give up acting altogether. "I love Ken and would do anything for him," he said to an interviewer; "but on a movie set

Richard Chamberlain as Tchaikovsky in *The Music Lovers*
(credit: United Artists).

he is so serious and demanding. That picture nearly put me in the loony bin. But I loved the film."[3]

Glenda Jackson, as Gudrun in *Women in Love*, had parodied Nina Milyukova's wretched marriage to Tchaikovsky while clowning with Loerke the homosexual. Now she took up the role of Nina in *The Music Lovers* in earnest. "Glenda Jackson is my kind of actress," Russell said at the time. "Some actresses talk about the character they are playing incessantly, but not Glenda; you have a preliminary discussion of the character with her and then she sticks to that throughout the shooting."

For her part, Glenda Jackson said in a radio interview that working with Russell is stimulating because "he creates the most incredible climate of genuine productivity. I'm never short of an idea when I am working with Ken. He likes you to offer suggestions, because vaguely one knows what he is looking for, the avenues he wants you to go down. He's a professional and he expects you to be the same."

The Music Lovers covers only two years in the composer's life, the period of this marriage, which was the turning point of his life. When the film begins Tchaikovsky is involved with the rich Vladimir Chiluvsky (Christopher Gable), whose possessiveness helps to turn Tchaikovsky's thoughts toward marriage, as does Tchaikovsky's long-cherished desire to have a family.

Tchaikovsky believes that man is governed by fate, and is in the midst of composing an opera on this theme entitled *Eugene Onegin*, in which a girl writes love letters to a man who turns her down, thereby ruining both his life and hers. Hence, when Tchaikovsky receives love letters from Nina Milyukova, he decides that the situation is too much of a coincidence to be ignored. He meets and marries Nina; and the marriage, of course, is a disaster, indicating how tragically misguided is Tchaikovsky's insistence in making life imitate art, instead of vice versa.

Nina also deceives herself, thinking that marrying a famous composer will automatically bring her happiness and prestige, with the result that the marriage renders Tchaikovsky an embittered neurotic and eventually drives his erstwhile wife into the asylum where she ends her days.

The chief source for the film is the biography of Catherine Drinker Bowen and Barbara von Meck, the daughter of

Tchaikovsky's patroness Madame Nadejda von Meck, which contains much of the florid thirteen-year correspondence between the composer and his patroness, who in point of fact never met. But Russell, with the help of screen writer Melvyn Bragg, veteran of several Russell BBC ventures, subjected the historical data to his own creative responses. As a result, film critics and moviegoers unfamiliar with Russell's highly imaginative TV biopics were considerably dismayed when *The Music Lovers* did not turn out to be the conventional screen biography of a composer which they had anticipated.

For example Russell amalgamates several of Tchaikovsky's male lovers into a single figure, Count Anton Chiluvsky, whose last name is a variation on the last name of one of those lovers, Vladimir Shilovsky. The opening credit of the film introduces "Ken Russell's film on Tchaikovsky and *The Music Lovers*," and for Russell, Chiluvsky is one of the possessive lovers of Tchaikovsky and his music with whom Tchaikovsky the man and the composer is involved in the course of the film; but there are others. These include Tchaikovsky's sister Sasha, whose relationship with her brother possesses an incestuous undercurrent; Madame von Meck, whose feeling for her protégé is something more than platonic; and Nina, the neurotic who becomes his wife.

Russell brings all of these individuals together at the premiere of Tchaikovsky's First Piano Concerto, though there is no evidence that any but Sasha actually attended this particular performance. Once Russell has assembled all of these characters whose lives are interwoven one way or another with Tchaikovsky's, however, the director can then proceed to examine these varied relationships for the balance of the film. Russell is masterly in the way that he cuts back and forth between the lives of these people, using Tchaikovsky's music as a bridge. This is nowhere better illustrated than in the sequence set at the premiere of the First Piano Concerto, in which Russell shows the daydreams which the piece inspires in its composer as he plays it and in Nina, whom Tchaikovsky has not yet met, as she listens.

As he plays the slow movement, Tchaikovsky recalls in sumptuously beautiful images the past summer that he spent with his married sister Sasha and her family, an idyllic interlude into which the figure of Chiluvsky intrudes. In this way

The Music Lovers, Tchaikovsky with two lovers: (top) a possessive man, Chiluvsky (Christopher Gable); (bottom) an ambitious woman, Nina (Glenda Jackson) (credits: Ken Russell and United Artists).

Russell brilliantly visualizes the conflict in Tchaikovsky's mind and heart between his wish to have a family and his homosexual tendencies.

For her part, Nina imagines herself marrying the handsome Russian officer who happens to be sitting near her at the concert. The pair are pictured galloping along in a carriage gleefully drinking champagne, accompanied by an appropriately elegant passage of the concerto. But the romantic illusions of both Tchaikovsky and Nina, which have been inspired by the composer's romantic music, are soon to be shattered; for life seldom lives up to the aspirations of art, Russell suggests.

To depict the spurious lyricism of the fantasies of Tchaikovsky and Nina, Russell employs soft-focus, slow-motion photography, and all of the other techniques which he learned to use while making television commercials to enhance prosaic reality. "The television commercial's trick of passing off a dream world as both a desirable and an attainable reality is one of the great tragedies of our age," he says. It is the twin tragedy of both Tchaikovsky and Nina that they too cling to a dream world that they insist, until it is too late, is both desirable and attainable. Russell says that the core of *The Music Lovers*, therefore, is the destructive force of dreams on people's lives.

The smashing of their stubborn illusion that their marriage can bring fulfillment to both of them occurs for Tchaikovsky and Nina in the famous railway carriage sequence of the film. The episode is based on one of Tchaikovsky's letters and thus represents an interesting example of how Russell's creative imagination can build skimpy factual data into a dramatic confrontation. In his letter Tchaikovsky records that when the train that was to take him and Nina on their honeymoon was about to leave the station, he was choked with sobs and even suppressed a scream at the very thought of a long journey in his bride's company. He consequently entertained her with conversation "to earn the right to lie in the dark in my own armchair, alone with myself."[4]

In the film this recollection becomes the traumatic experience of a homosexual locked in a private compartment with his drunkenly amorous wife, whose disrobing revolts rather than entices him. The carriage rocks back and forth like a storm-tossed ship as it hurtles through the snowy night; and Tchaikovsky's sweating face, illumined solely by a swaying lamp overhead, twists into fear and revulsion at the sight of the grotesque creature that seems about to devour him.

In shooting this scene Russell used a technique borrowed from the days of silent films, that of having mood music played on the set while a particularly difficult scene was being shot. Although the railway carriage scene would eventually be scored to Tchaikovsky's *Pathetique* Symphony and the Manfred Tone Poem, the director chose a notably frenzied, barbaric passage from Shostakovich's Execution of Stephan Razin Cantata and had it blared over loudspeakers surrounding the railway compartment set. Since the scene took two days to shoot, Russell asked Glenda Jackson at one point if the music was driving her mad; she replied that if he stopped the music she could not do the scene at all. During the duration of shooting that scene, Russell remembers, she and Chamberlain, as well as the crew, were all totally enslaved to the rhythms of that Shostakovich piece. Meanwhile Russell had captured one of the most overwhelming scenes in the entire film.

A movie that generates as much tension as this one does needs some comic relief, and Russell shrewdly provides it, sometimes at the least likely moments. After an ugly quarrel with Nina over his psychological impotency, Tchaikovsky storms out of the house and heads for the river bank where he means to drown himself. He leaps into the water—only to find to his chagrin that it is but knee-deep. As a female passerby titters at the sight of a grown man childishly splashing about in the shallow water along the shore, Tchaikovsky realizes that he is a flop even at taking his own life.

The real-life Tchaikovsky was aware that the river was shallow at the point where he jumped in; but his intention was to expose himself to the icy waters long enough to contract pneumonia and therefore die apparently of natural causes, thus concealing his suicide. Russell chooses to make Tchaikovsky's suicide attempt in the film look foolish, however, in order to present it as the culminating episode in what Tchaikovsky sees as the unbroken series of failures permeating his life. Not only is his marriage a farce, but his best compositions are ignored in favor of his crowd-pleasing program music like the March Slav. At this point of the film, therefore, Tchaikovsky's failure at suicide is the capstone of his failure in both the personal and professional sectors of his life.

Russell's handling of the suicide episode, then, is typical of the way he adapts the precise details of a person's life to suit his dramatic intent, in order to dramatize the individual's life in the most effective way possible. By the same token Russell draws a dramatic parallel between Tchaikovsky's attempt at suicide by drowning and his later drinking of a glass of unsterilized water during a cholera epidemic, which leads to his death from cholera. For Russell both actions stem from the same death wish which the composer nurtured throughout his later life.

Tchaikovsky did contract cholera and die from it, but there is no direct evidence that his intention in drinking the unsterilized water was suicidal. Yet it is quite plausible that a man who had tried to kill himself once would at least subconsciously do it again. Moreover, Russell roots the suicidal aspect of Tchaikovsky's death in the fact that the composer's mother died of cholera and that his close attachment to her in life had spawned the lifelong obsession that his death would parallel hers.

Russell concretizes Tchaikovsky's traumatic memory of his mother's death in a fantasy sequence in which Tchaikovsky recalls himself as a boy hysterically trying to extricate his mortally ill mother from the grip of two medical attendants who are immersing her in the scalding waters of a steaming tub in a misguided and futile attempt to cure her of cholera. In point of fact Tchaikovsky did not witness the death of his mother in real life because he was out of the city at the time of her death. What Russell is establishing in this fantasy sequence, however, is the deep-seated emotional attachment which the real Tchaikovsky did cherish for his mother and which made her untimely death a shattering experience for the lad.

It is a commonplace fact among Tchaikovsky's biographers that he adored his mother to a degree that exceeded by far the normal feelings of a son for a mother and that this element in his personality helped to ground his homosexuality; and her death left him chronically melancholy and haunted by the notion that he would some day perish as she did—as in fact he eventually did. Russell has cut across these facts in his film and meshed them in a way that is true to Tchaikovsky's psyche if not completely accurate in historical detail. Furthermore the visual shorthand which he employs in the fantasy sequence about the death of Tchaikovsky's mother does enable the viewer to grasp more fully the psychological basis in Tchaikovsky's youth for his behavior as an adult.

Indeed, the fantasy sequences with which Russell often punctuates his biopics are a clear indication that the director wants to explore the character and personality of the subjects about whom he makes biographical films, and not merely to document on film the historical facts of their lives. Even Pauline Kael, the most acerbic American critic of Russell's biopics, concedes in her review of *The Music Lovers* that the Hollywood biographical films of the past simplified character and in other ways altered the lives of their subjects.

The Great Victor Herbert in 1939, for instance, invented a whole fictional subplot that had almost nothing at all to do with the composer himself, just to make his dull life of composing successful operettas more interesting for the mass audience. It would seem that the same kind of poetic license that the old Hollywood biographies enjoyed should be extended to Russell in order to allow him to illuminate the personalities as well as the lives of the subjects of his biopics. After all, his highly imaginative approach to his material is a clear tip-off that he is presenting his own interpretation of an artist's private life and public accomplishments, an interpretation which the viewer is free to accept or reject.

In addition, it would seem that Russell should be as free as any official biographer to speculate about the gaps in the known facts of a historical figure's life. It is an accepted fact, for example, that in 1890 Madame von Meck abruptly terminated her patronage of Tchaikovsky; but no one knows for certain why she did so. Russell postulates a plausible explanation in what is perhaps the most perfectly realized visual symbol in the entire movie.

This occurs in the scene in which Madame von Meck gives a birthday party in Tchaikovsky's honor. As he and her children dance amid a dazzling display of fireworks, Chiluvsky, who is jealous of Tchaikovsky's marriage to Nina and of his relationship with his wealthy patroness, cruelly tells Madame von

Meck of Tchaikovsky's homosexuality, just as a likeness of the
composer made of fireworks lights up the sky. As Chiluvsky
finishes his revelation and Madame von Meck turns away
from him with a cynical smile on her face, the image in the sky
dwindles into darkness. It is not surprising that, soon after, she
withdraws her financial support from Tchaikovsky, for Russell
has already symbolically pictured her disillusionment at dis-
covering that the man with whom she was secretly infatuated
is homosexual.

The sudden loss of his patroness leads Modeste, Tchaikovsky's brother and business manager, to suggest that he go on
tour conducting his own works in order to raise both his spirits
and his bank balance. Russell portrays the triumphant tour as a
spectacular fantasy sequence, scored to the 1812 Overture.
While Tchaikovsky is shown being carried aloft on the shoul-
ders of his adoring public amid a swirl of streamers and
money, Modeste busily and greedily collects the bills in a
sack; he then sets off several salvos from a cannon which de-
capitate one by one the possessive lovers of Tchaikovsky and
his music while they sit together in a concert-hall box watching the maestro conduct. Chiluvsky, Sasha, and Madame von
Meck are all thus disposed of.

A shot of Tchaikovsky waving his baton exultantly dissolves
to a shot of a stone statue of the composer-conductor frozen in
the same gesture with snowflakes falling around it. The implication of this fantasy sequence is that Tchaikovsky has become
financially independent and famous and can now afford to remain aloof from those with whom his life was formerly involved. But life on a pedestal can be cold and lonely; and his
despondency for having traded on his talent for crass, commercial success, as well as the continued nagging of his unresolved sexual conflicts, leads to his drinking the infected
water that masochistically precipitates his dying from cholera
in the same manner as did his mother, the only woman he ever
loved.

The last image of the film, however, is not of Tchaikovsky
but of his wretched estranged wife staring blankly through the
bars of her padded cell. Russell has been criticized for gratuit-
ously inserting grotesque scenes of Nina's internment in a
madhouse near the end of the picture, since in reality Nina
was not committed to an insane asylum until three years after

her ex-husband's death. But these scenes are in the film to make a point: after selfishly marrying Nina to squelch gossip about his homosexuality, Tchaikovsky later callously abandoned her to the living nightmare of a nineteenth-century asylum.

For me one of the most heartbreaking moments in the film occurs when Nina, wandering in her madness, experiences a moment of lucidity in which she clearly realizes that, contrary to all of her romantic delusions, her husband never loved her. This unbearably painful thought drives her into a hysterical fit until she is subdued in a strait jacket, a symbol of how her emotional and sexual life was strait-jacketed by her marriage to a homosexual whose revulsion for her accelerated the disturbed young woman's rapid decline into promiscuity, prostitution, and insanity.

Stephen Farber perfectly sums up Russell's final criticism of Tchaikovsky when he writes that Tchaikovsky leaves Nina to retreat into the romantic world of his music, where he is in full control and where he can sublimate his emotional frustration into art; but his rejection of Nina destroys her. "His music survives at her expense."[5] Nevertheless Russell's purpose in presenting Tchaikovsky in this unflattering light is not to denigrate or deromanticize his music, but to criticize the man who wrote it, and to indicate the price that he and others paid for its creation.

The Devils (1971)

Filmgoers who were unsettled by Russell's treatment of Tchaikovsky in *The Music Lovers* were even more unprepared for Russell's baroque rendering of the story of religious conflicts in seventeenth century France, which Russell based on Aldous Huxley's book *The Devils of Loudon* and John Whiting's play *The Devils*. Before shooting began, Russell had this to say about his film version of *The Devils*:

I used all of the available documentation, but I had to thin it out because it is so vast. The story is based on the same historical incident which served as the basis of Kawalerowicz's 1961 Polish film, *Mother Joan of the Angels*, which I saw about five years ago. But my version of the story will bring in more of the political background of the period than did the Polish film. Also my Catholic background helps me to distinguish between normal religious practices and the bizarre things attributed to the nuns in *The Devils*. Since Kawalerowicz is not a Christian, the whole idea of convent life would seem bizarre to him. The film has some things to say about the Church of that period, but the Church will survive it.

At any rate I don't mind now if I am able to make the film or not since I have worked it out shot by shot in my imagination. I can run it in my head any time I want to. Although I must admit a finished film is often very different from the way one has initially pictured it in one's mind.

The central character of *The Devils* is Father Urbain Grandier, who leads the people of the city of Loudon in opposition to Cardinal Richelieu's plan to destroy the city walls which make their city independent of the crown and therefore able to resist Richelieu's effort to centralize the French government. Richelieu's minions take advantage of the fact that Grandier is known to have been guilty of several sexual indiscretions and accuse him of having corrupted, as Satan's agent, an entire convent of Ursuline nuns, starting with the prioress, Mother Jeanne. In the ensuing hysteria, Grandier is tried, convicted, and burned at the stake; and the city walls are reduced to rubble.

"What particularly drew me to the subject matter of *The Devils*," said Russell, "was the fact that it reflected an instance of the collision of the individual with the State. We know from history that the State usually survives while the individual loses out in these cases; but I wanted to examine what lasting impact the individual still has, even when he loses."

Russell had trouble getting backing for the film after United Artists turned it down. After four months of shopping around, Warners agreed to sponsor the project. He had hoped to reunite two of the stars of *Women in Love*, with Oliver Reed as Grandier and Glenda Jackson as Sister Jeanne. Oliver Reed accepted the part of Grandier; but Glenda Jackson refused to play Sister Jeanne, probably because Russell had had to curtail Sister Jeanne's role somewhat because of the excessive length of the original screenplay. Russell decided to end the film with the death of Grandier, whereas he had originally intended to go on to picture Sister Jeanne's notoriety as a spurious stigmatic. With this latter material out of the picture Glenda Jackson lost interest in the role.

The Devils: (top) Vanessa Redgrave as the bedeviled Sister Jeanne; (bottom), Father Grandier (Oliver Reed) harangues the citizens of the walled city of Loudon (credits: Movie Star News).

Vanessa Redgrave was chosen to costar with Oliver Reed instead, and the picture went into production in the fall of 1970, with principal photography completed by the end of the year. *The Devils* was released the following summer to a storm of indignation. When the movie was shown at the Venice Film Festival, the Patriarch of Venice (later Pope John Paul I) took it to task for visualizing on the screen "excesses never seen before," and the Vatican newspaper *L'Osservatore Romano* added that it did not wish to criticize the subject matter of the film so much as its depiction of the sexual violence and blasphemy with which it deals. The nonreligious press echoed these judgments of the movie, exclaiming that this time Russell had really gone too far.

Discussing the film in the wake of this avalanche of hostile criticism, Russell maintained that for him *The Devils* turned out to be exactly what he had intended it to be, a Christian film about a sinner who becomes a saint. Like Tchaikovsky, Grandier wants to achieve a more noble level of existence, but he is more capable of self-transcendence than was the composer, who remained self-indulgent to the end, in that Grandier is ultimately regenerated by the suffering he is forced to undergo.

"Grandier," according to Russell, "is a mixture of good and bad qualities; he knows what he should do, but he often doesn't do it, as St. Paul once said. Then he gets the opportunity to stand up against Richelieu in order to preserve the rights of the city and he does so. In this crisis his good qualities come to the surface and he dies a Christian martyr for his people."

Asked about the vividness with which he portrayed the bizarre events in *The Devils*, Russell replies,

Once I had decided to do *The Devils*, I had to go along with the truth as it was reported. I had to show the violent atmosphere that the plague had created at the time, for instance, in order to explain how ordinary people could stand by and allow a man they knew to be innocent to die a hideous death. They had become calloused as the result of the plague. When there is death on every doorstep, the death of a single man like Grandier becomes inconsequential, an everyday occurrence. That is why the crowd behaved at his burning as if they were attending a football match.

The picture is a jolly sight less ugly than Aldous Huxley's book. When one reads these events in Huxley's account, one can sift the

words through one's imagination and filter out as much of the un-
pleasantness as one cares to. You can't do this when you are looking at
a film. I was reading another book of Huxley's, his anti-Utopian novel
Ape and Essence, and I said to myself, this is ugly stuff, and were I to
film it people would probably say that I had exaggerated the presentation of the material of that book; but it really couldn't be exaggerated.

Joseph Gomez spends almost a quarter of his book on Russell's films in analyzing *The Devils* in the light of the historical
and literary sources which lie behind it, such as the Huxley
account and the Whiting play. Because of the negative reaction which the film prompted, Gomez obviously feels that he
had to take some pains in proving the serious intent of the
movie. Perhaps because I have never doubted that *The Devils*
was a motion picture of substance and merit, however, I find
Gomez's treatment of the film a bit too lengthy; but there is no
doubt that the movie and its sources deserve careful analysis;
and Gomez's conclusions about Russell's employment of Huxley and Whiting are surely valid.

Basically Gomez sees Huxley's book as fundamentally a
study of Grandier's quest for self-transcendence presented in
the context of the political, historical, and religious milieu in
which he lived; whereas Whiting's play, although based on
Huxley's book, centers more on the personal drama of Grandier's self-deception and self-destruction, "and the contrast between his method and that of Sister Jeanne in seeking a meaning to life."[6]

What Russell did in creating his screenplay was to take elements from both the book and the play which appealed to him
and blend them into a single coherent work. The personal religious drama of Grandier's rising above his self-destructive
behavior as a degenerate and worldly priest in order to attain
the self-transcendence of a martyr's death Russell took over
from Whiting's play; but he presented this drama in terms of
the larger historical and political background which Huxley
provides in his book. Russell was therefore able to use many of
the dramatic situations and much of the dialogue from the play
in his script, while at the same time he employed the historical
and political scope of Huxley's study as the meaningful frame
of reference against which Grandier's individual tragedy is
played out.

The historical context of the film is announced at the very beginning with a printed statement that "this film is based on historical fact. The principal characters lived and the major events depicted in the film actually took place." As in *The Music Lovers* Russell felt free to invent some minor events to fill out his presentation of the major ones; but even these, he would insist, grow as much out of what we know about the behavior of these historical characters and the temper of the times as out of his creative imagination.

The precredit sequence of the film, for example, is grounded in what is known about King Louis XIII: that he was, as Russell puts it, "an extravagant homosexual who loved dressing up in drag for court entertainments as much as he hated Protestants." The prologue contains both of these elements. The king (Graham Armitage) is seen rising from a seashell and cavorting about the stage in a very abbreviated costume as he enacts the birth of Venus. At the end of his number, he is applauded by his transvestite courtiers. This high camp opening of the film not only portrays the general decadence of Louis and his court, but also presages the side-show atmosphere of the public exorcisms to be practiced on Sister Jeanne and the other members of her convent later in the movie.

A serious note is struck amid the levity of the scene when Richelieu (Christopher Logue) comes forth to express his patronizing approval of the king's performance of the birth of Venus and adds that he hopes that he and the king will be able to collaborate on the birth of a new France, in which Church and State will join forces to drive the Protestant from the land. The shot of Richelieu and the king freezes on the screen, and the title of the film is superimposed on their faces. This is Russell's way of showing that, in their collusion to gain their own selfish political goals, Cardinal Richelieu and King Louis are the real devils at work in the film.

They are abetted in their schemes to destroy Grandier by some lesser demons. Baron de Laubardemont and Father Mignon, as representatives of king and cardinal, meet with Philippe Trincant, whom Grandier has seduced and abandoned, and her father in order to fabricate testimony that will support Sister Jeanne's allegations that Grandier has corrupted her entire convent. The girl and her father, of course, are willing to help in any plan by which they can get revenge on Grandier, and de Laubardemont and Mignon are bent on currying favor with Louis and Richelieu. As they meet in secret to carry on their plotting, the scene is lit by the flickering flames of a fire which suggests that they are conniving in some murky corner of hell.

Elsewhere in the film Russell also places his characters in settings that comment visually on their character or behavior. Sister Jeanne is frequently photographed in a small room or in a narrow corridor or through a grating to imply how she is imprisoned by her neurotic fantasies. Moreover, the physical deformity of Sister Jeanne, who is humpbacked, symbolizes her spiritual deformity, which in turn gives rise to her religio-sexual fantasies about Grandier.

These fantasies present Grandier as identified with Christ and herself with Mary Magdalene, for in this way she subconsciously seeks to disguise her physical lust for the priest as spiritual love of Christ. In one of these fantasies in the film, Sister Jeanne sees herself as Magdalene at the foot of Christ's cross on Calvary, and Grandier as the crucified Christ hanging on the cross. Russell photographs this sequence, in which Grandier descends from the cross to accept Sister Jeanne's fevered embraces, in black-and-white, thereby calling to mind Cecil B. de Mille's biblical epics. This particular dream vision of Sister Jeanne's recalls in particular Cecil B. de Mille's *King of Kings*, which was as preoccupied with the sins of Magdalene as with the virtues of Christ. As Jack Fisher notes in treating *The Devils*, Russell's parodying of de Mille at this point is especially appropriate because, like Sister Jeanne's fantasies, de Mille's religious movies "usually teetered on the edge of the obscene. The more religious his films were, the more they teetered."[7]

One undisputed virtue of de Mille's spectacles is also to be found in *The Devils* — not that Russell was necessarily influenced by de Mille on this point; it is simply a quality that their historical films have in common. It is their ability to "personalize" a crowd scene by focusing on individuals within the group in the course of the sequence. This directorial touch is based on the sound assumption that audiences cannot identify with an anonymous crowd but only with individuals who are participants in the crowd. Russell uses this effect to best advantage in the scenes of Sister Jeanne's public exorcism.

By this point in the film the nuns of Sister Jeanne's convent are convinced that they too are infected by the demons which Grandier has supposedly unleashed in Sister Jeanne. They are therefore easily stirred up into a frenzy by the carnival atmosphere of Sister Jeanne's exorcism, and Russell captures their individual torment by intercutting long shots of the mass hysteria with close shots of the contorted faces of individual nuns. The overall atmosphere of the scene may be chaotic, but Russell's handling of it is not.

Discussions of *The Devils* which deal almost exclusively with such scenes as the one just described tend to give the impression that the film proceeds relentlessly from one scene of grotesque horror to another. In point of fact *The Devils* contains some of the most subdued and lyrical passages which Russell has ever filmed, scenes which are deliberately designed as a contrast to the wild aberrations protrayed elsewhere in the movie.

The most outstanding example of this kind of scene is the one in which Grandier is returning to Loudon from an audience with the king, convinced that he must, like Joan of Arc, sacrifice himself for his people even if this sacrifice may be misunderstood by friend and foe alike. He breaks his journey to offer Mass in the natural splendor of a roadside oasis. Afterward he continues on his way, firm in the conviction that he can at last accomplish some good in his wasted life by saving the city from falling under the dictatorial sway of Richelieu and that God will accept his sufferings at the hands of his political enemies in atonement for his past sins. "I know what I have sown and I am prepared to reap accordingly," he muses.

"Despite Grandier's faults as a man, he is also a priest," Russell comments. "I wanted to show at this point in the film the distinction between the office and the man: the man may be personally unworthy of his priestly office and yet at times still be able to rise to the demands of that office."

Novelist Graham Greene once wrote that a thin line separates the sinner from the saint, and it is that line which Grandier crosses when he dies a martyr's death. "The greatest saints have been men with more than a normal capacity for evil, and the most vicious men have sometimes narrowly avoided sanctity," he concludes.[8]

Grandier's regeneration is contrasted with Sister Jeanne's remaining firmly entrenched in her religious and sexual neuroses. "Look on me and learn the meaning of love," Grandier, disfigured by torture, shouts to her on his way to his death. He wants her to confront her sins as he has finally come to terms with his. But she cannot or will not, for her twisted love of him has long since turned to hatred. "You devil!" she hisses at him in a rasping voice. Her remark is ironic because, as I mentioned earlier, the real devils are king and cardinal, not the regenerated priestly martyr.

Grandier's dying at the stake like Joan of Arc is surely one of the most realistically filmed deaths by fire ever recorded on film. Through the flames Grandier's face can be seen purpling and blistering until he is completely enveloped in a wall of fire. This image led London critic Alexander Walker to note in his review of the film that the makeup man alone deserves praise for his work on *The Devils*. Walker's review also took Russell to task for such anachronisms as that of Louis XIII quipping after he shoots a Protestant prisoner dressed in a blackbird costume, "Bye-bye, Blackbird."

For Russell this ludicrous allusion to a Twenties pop tune is part of the overall intent of this scene to point up the outrageous behavior of Louis, who casually executes political prisoners as part of his target practice. The anachronistically modern sets, however, have another explanation. The cathedral, the convent, and the government buildings are not edifices of gray medieval stone, but sleek, all-white buildings which tower above the city. The modern architecture is meant to emphasize once again Russell's point, made earlier in this chapter, that people living in the past thought of themselves as contemporary in the same way that we think of ourselves as contemporary. The modern settings, consequently, help to give more immediacy to the religious and political issues dealt with in the picture.

Although critical feeling about the film was negative at the time it was released, subsequent essays in film journals about *The Devils* have emphasized its serious intent. Certainly *The Devils* is Russell's most overtly religious film and clearly re-

flects the thematic elements of sin, love, faith, guilt, forgiveness, and redemption which he feels comprise the "Catholic
outlook" of his films and which one way or another figure in
virtually all of his motion pictures.

Grandier accomplished his redemption by a self-transcendence achieved through his noble death. The hero of Russell's
next biopic, Henri Gaudier, lived and died in a much less
melodramatic way than Grandier; yet Russell in many ways
esteems him much more.

Savage Messiah (1972)

Because Russell is, in Colin Wilson's phrase, a director in
search of a hero, it was inevitable that he would commit
Gaudier's life to film. As I mentioned in the first chapter, Russell has admired Gaudier from his youth, when he first picked
up *Savage Messiah*, H. S. Ede's biography of the struggling
young sculptor who died at twenty-three in World War I.

"I first read the book when I was struggling to get started in
my own career," Russell remembers.

I was given new courage to carry on by an account of a young art
student who refused to give up his aspirations despite adversity. I
was also touched by his love for Sophie Brzeska, a disillusioned
Polish woman twenty years his senior. It was the story of two people
who were devoted to each other in a brother-sister relationship which
they never consummated sexually, and how she sank into despair
after his untimely death, and eventually was committed to a lunatic
asylum. I was attracted to this material because Gaudier was not what
the general public considered an artist to be. He wasn't someone
special tucked away at the top of an ivory tower making works which
were totally obscure, to be admired by a few friends. He was somebody working for posterity and eternity, somebody who felt that there
was something in him which he could transmit to his fellow human
beings which might be of use to them. In short, I wanted to make a
film of his life that would be a tribute to him for the inspiration which
he had given me when I needed it.

Ede's book was the result of his piecing together the jour-
nals which Sophie Brzeska had written about her life with
Gaudier during her last years in the mental institution.
"Sophie always held herself responsible for Gaudier's death,"
Russell explains. "She felt that if she had married him, he

would not have been so reckless in the war. In her last letter to him she once more refused his marriage proposal, and he was killed soon after that. She began to wander the streets of London, madly insisting that he was still alive, and ended up in an asylum, where she died of pneumonia in 1925—still accusing herself of his death and leaving behind a rambling journal of their life together."

Ede's book does draw on Sophie's diary, but given the diary's highly personal and at times incoherent style, he depends more heavily on Gaudier's letters to Sophie, for which he has provided a running commentary. Russell attempted to buy the rights to Ede's book while he was still working at the BBC, but was told that they had already been purchased by an American producer. Then, in 1971, Ede wrote to Russell informing him that the American producer's option had lapsed, and Russell purchased the film rights immediately.

Russell believed in the project of making a film of Gaudier's life to the extent of investing in the production himself. "Otherwise it would have taken me much longer to finance the film," he says. "I then set out to make the film as good as possible for as little as possible." Because Russell has found that the smaller the budget a film has, the less likely the front office is to interfere with its production, he trimmed the budget for *Savage Messiah* to just below $750,000 and shot the film in a small studio which he jokingly refers to as a "derelict biscuit factory on the banks of a stagnant canal. But it served my purposes and kept the overhead down. It also recalled the old days at the BBC of working with a small unit and a short shooting schedule, as' did having Dick Bush as cinematographer for the first time since the days of *Isadora* and *Delius*."

In a letter which he wrote before shooting began he said, "*Savage Messiah* will be more like *Delius* than *The Devils*. Dorothy Tutin and an unknown boy fresh out of the Royal Academy of Dramatic Arts named Scott Antony are the stars."[9] He later elaborated on his central casting of the picture, saying that it was hard to find a young actor of twenty "who could actually pick up a hammer and chisel, and reduce a six-foot piece of marble to the size of a pea"; but it was important that the individual who played Gaudier could appear to sculpt, just as it was important that the actor who played Tchaikovsky in *The Music Lovers* could do a credible job of playing a piano.

Savage Messiah: Scott Antony as the sculptor Henri Gaudier.

Gaudier with Sophie Brzeska (Dorothy Tutin) (credits: Ken Russell).

"I finally found Scott Antony," Russell says, "and in his screen tests I made him get hold of a hammer and chisel and smash something. I had to believe that he could produce the work that Gaudier produced, and he did make me believe it."

Casting Sophie Brzeska was no easier a task than casting Gaudier. Russell's budget could not afford the salary of a Jeanne Moreau; and other actresses would not agree to being made to look sufficiently unglamorous for the role. "Then I remembered a wonderful, fantastic actress I had seen on the English stage twenty years ago, Dorothy Tutin. No one ever gave her a real break in films; and so she only played bit parts, although her stage career had gone forward in glowing style. So I got Dorothy Tutin to make her real screen debut in a key part twenty years later than it should have been."

Dorothy Tutin found working with Russell somewhat trying at times, but always rewarding. There was one exterior scene in which she was to wear a huge, wide-brimmed hat which flapped in the wind while she played the scene; and she was irritated when Russell refused to let her pin it on her head so that it would not prove a distraction when she was speaking her lines. Russell told her instead to hold the hat on her head with her hand if need be; and in this way he got the effect that he wanted, for Dorothy Tutin's irritation and distraction about the hat helped to suggest Sophie's restless, insecure state of mind.

When she saw the scene on the screen, she realized that the trust which she had placed in Russell all along had been justified. "You feel that he knows *exactly* what the film will be like," she comments; "it was often a question of catching up with Ken and his conception of the film."[10]

Russell's conception of a biopic develops gradually, starting with the period when he is doing research on the subject of the movie. He reads voraciously and consults authorities in the field until "there comes a moment when everything you know about him crystallizes; and right or wrong, you know that's how it's got to be."[11]

While doing background research for *Savage Messiah*, Russell came to realize that the source of the mutual attraction of Henri Gaudier and Sophie Brzeska is that their contrasting personalities complement each other. "Sophie and Henri are very different in many ways," he points out. "Henri is exuberant and impetuous, Sophie is more genteel and mature. The one thing that draws them together is their mutual loneliness. Their complicated relationship is partially that of a mother and son, of a sister and brother, and of two lovers, though Sophie refuses to allow Henri to make love to her or to marry her because she has been deserted more than once by a suitor in the past." But they reinforce the bond between them by combining their last names into Gaudier-Brzeska.

Russell establishes the nature of their relationship in the opening scene of the movie, in which Henri meets Sophie for the first time in the public library. His boyishly aggressive, warm good humor gradually melts her cool reserve, and two shy people desperate for companionship gradually make contact with one another.

Henri playfully makes a toy bird from paper and hands it to Sophie, and she smiles in spite of herself. Then he leans over and whispers disarmingly, "I'm lonely; are you?" "Of course I am," she blurts out, surprised at her own candor; and they leave the library together. The tentative, touching way that these two people meet ranks among the gentlest scenes Russell has ever created, and is matched in tenderness by the later scene in which the hand of the young man is shown in close-up clasped in that of the older woman, representing the first time that they both feel secure enough to demonstrate their affection for one another. This image reminds one that during the credits Henri was shown sketching one of his own hands. Now his lone hand has a mate to enfold it.

Given the exquisite scenes just described, it is difficult to understand Pauline Kael's complaint in her review of the film that the director never dramatizes for the audience the source of the mutual attraction of Henri and Sophie. Not only does he suggest the inner loneliness that is assuaged by their companionship, but he also displays the external forces that serve to drive them together. Both Henri and Sophie in their own way are eccentrics who at times arouse hostility and ridicule in those who do not understand them, but rarely inspire friendship and acceptance in others. Hence their need for each other.

Russell places a scene early in the film that symbolically shows their concomitant need to stand together against an uncomprehending and oppressive society which rejects their nonconformist behavior and outlook. Henri gets so excited in elaborating for Sophie his revolutionary concept of art that he climbs atop a statue in a public park to declaim his ideas to the bystanders until the police chase him and Sophie away.

The rejection of the pair's unconventional ideas is matched by the parallel rejection of their unconventional relationship. During a visit to his parents in the country, Henri arranges to have Sophie stay in a cottage near his parents' home; but she is forced to vacate the premises because of complaints (secretly lodged by Henri's mother) about Sophie's "improper reception of men" during her stay in the cottage. This is painfully ironic since Sophie's "reception of men" has consisted of holding hands with Henri.

Exasperated by this treatment of Sophie, he takes her to live in London. As they embark for the big city, Russell shows them disappearing down a country lane (symbolic of the new road which their lives are taking), while Henri looks up at the thunder clouds overhead and utters a prayer that his Father in heaven will help them to find a sanctuary in London. If Sophie is a mother-figure for Henri, Nature itself seems to be his pantheistic father-figure, since he often addresses the heavens as Father.

Once in London the hapless pair can only afford a squalid basement flat to live in; but they become acquainted with a bohemian group of art fanciers who pretentiously style themselves as the Vorticists, presided over by a decadent, lubricious art dealer named Lionel Shaw (John Justin). Shaw's condescenion drives the impulsive Henri to boast rashly about a new work in stone which he has just completed, and Shaw casually agrees to come by Henri's flat the following morning to view it. Actually Henri has not even begun the piece which he described to Shaw, and therefore he is forced to make good his boast by stealing a tombstone from a graveyard as raw material and then working all night to fashion it into the statue which he described to Shaw.

It was this sequence in particular which Russell had in mind when he said that the actor he chose to play Henri would have to look convincing when he was wielding a sculpture's hammer and chisel. Russell had always wanted to make the point that in one or another of his biopics that creating any work of art requires perspiration as well as inspiration, and decided that a sculptor was the most appropriate kind of artist to use in order to communicate this concept to an audience. Therefore, in this sense, this scene is not only the key sequence in *Savage Messiah*, but is thematically central to all of Russell's biopics about great artists, be they sculptors, composers, or painters.

While Henri is working through the night, carving his statue, he keeps himself alert by discoursing on his philosophy of art to Sophie and their friend Corky, who doze intermittently throughout the long night's vigil. Henri's monologue completely captures the spirit of the young artist without trying to offer any facile explanation of his work. "The stone leads you," Henri comments. "Every blow of the hammer is a risk. It's as much a mystery to the one who is doing the sculpture as to the one who looks at it." He continues, "There's no such thing as an artist who doesn't need an audience. If he doesn't, he is more of a saint than an artist. Don't believe that solitary genius stuff. If what I do doesn't please me, how will it give anything to anyone else?"

When morning comes Shaw does not bother to show up to look at Henri's work. The bohemian world, as much as the philistines of the middle class, it seems, care not at all for Henri and his work. He gets even with Shaw for this keenly felt slight, however, by transporting the statue in a wheelbarrow to Shaw's gallery and heaving it through the display window.

Gaudier's luck changes, however, when he gets the chance to do a one-man exhibition. He loses himself in his work, and when one of the Vorticists visits him while he is busy sculpting and chides him for not joining the army to fight the enemy, he retorts acidly, "Those who speak of enemies are my enemies." She jeeringly calls him an ill-bred savage who thinks himself a messiah. As Henri chips away, the dust from the stone which he is carving sprinkles his hair gray, giving him the appearance of growing older. As a matter of fact Henri is becoming more mature, and is taking life more seriously.

One day he reaches through the grating that separates him from the rest of the world while he is sculpting in his basement area and buys a newspaper. It tells him that Rheims Cathedral and other monuments of art and architecture which he cherishes are being destroyed in the war. He therefore decides to set his work aside and to go off to join the army in order to preserve the culture that he loves. Russell sketches Henri's life and death at the front during World War I very simply. A single photograph of Henri in uniform, smiling as he holds up a madonna which he has carved on a rifle handle, is all that we see of his military experience.

As for his death, that is reported to Shaw and his cronies as they chuckle indulgently over Henri's latest letter from the trenches boisterously airing his patriotic sentiments. Someone says, "Whoever wrote that should be shot!" Corky responds quietly, "He was; last Thursday."

After his death the exhibition which Henri was preparing at the time he joined the army is held posthumously. The camera examines pieces of sculpture which the viewer has seen Henri creating at various times in the course of the film, and then cuts to Sophie in the basement flat which she shared with Henri. She is weeping softly as she stands before the unfinished statue on which Henri was working the day that he decided to enlist. She is of course oblivious to the victory parade passing by outside. After Sophie takes her last leave of the now abandoned flat, the camera comes to rest on the unfinished statue, tragic symbol of Henri's unrealized potential.

Savage Messiah is Russell's most mellow, understated biographical feature film. He depicts neither the death of Henri nor the commitment of Sophie to a lunatic asylum—whereas in *The Music Lovers* he portrayed both Tchaikovsky's hideous death from cholera and Nina's equally appalling deterioration in the mental institution. This is not a matter of inconsistency on Russell's part. Russell portrayed Nina's madness because he believed that Tchaikovsky to some degree had been partially responsible for Nina's insanity by his calloused and insensitive treatment of her. On the other hand, there is no such link between Henri's behavior and Sophie's insanity. By the same token Russell had a purpose in portraying Tchaikovsky's death because of its tie-in with the death of the composer's mother and with his earlier attempt at suicide, as I pointed out in my treatment of *Music Lovers*. But Henri's death is a simple, straightforward act of courage with no such murky implications underlying it, and is best shown from the point of view of those who do not appreciate his self-sacrifice any more than they appreciated his art, in order to increase the viewer's sympathy for him.

"In the last analysis," Russell explains, "*Savage Messiah* called for a more quiet, subdued kind of film treatment than did *The Music Lovers*. The style of each of my films is dictated by the subject matter. I took one quarrel scene out of *Savage Messiah* during the editing process. It may have happened in real life, but it was too powerful for the overall tone of the film, because the movie runs about a hundred minutes and not several years, which is the period covered by the story."

Very much in keeping with Russell's controlled directorial style throughout the picture is the scene by the sea, in which Henri and Sophie joyously cavort along the shore, celebrating their companionship. Suddenly Henri leaps barefoot onto a rock and euphorically exults about his artistic talent and his hopes for realizing it, and then repeats once more his marriage proposal to Sophie. He is brought back to earth with a severe jolt, however, when she rejects his proposal yet again. He limps away across the beach like a wounded bird, as if feeling the pebbles under his feet for the first time.

Russell has brilliantly captured here the difference between Henri the artist and Henri the human being. As an artist Henri is self-sufficient and towers above Sophie and the others in their circle, just as he stands above her on the rock. But as a person Henri is in many ways a vulnerable little boy much in need of emotional support, as evidenced by his moping sulkily away at the end of the scene.

This distinction between the artist and the man is one that Russell is at pains to draw in every one of his biopics, in order to show how the artist can transcend his limitations as a flawed human being and produce great art. There is no doubt that Russell admires how Henri did this in his short life. Gustav Mahler, on the other hand, would seem to fall far shorter than Gaudier of anything like heroic stature in Russell's view, judging by Russell's film about the Austrian composer.

Mahler (1974)

Russell places Mahler more or less in the same category with Tchaikovsky as a man who had no qualms about subordinating his wife's life and personal interests to his own. Since Alma Mahler, unlike Nina Tchaikovsky, was not emotionally disturbed, she was not crushed in the way that Nina was by

her husband's self-aggrandizing ways. Nonetheless, Russell
implies in the Mahler film that Mahler was responsible for the
atrophy of his wife's own admittedly lesser potential for musical composition because he demanded that she devote herself
entirely to helping him further his career.

Because Anna Mahler suspected that a Russell film about
her father would be critical of his life and personality, she initially declined Russell's request for permission to make the
movie. She replied to his inquiry that she had not been
pleased by *The Music Lovers* and would prefer not to have a
Russell film made about her father. Russell responded that in
his Tchaikovsky film he was trying to analyze how a composer
must transcend the problems that confront him in his personal
life in order to write great music and then tactfully suggested
that she see *The Music Lovers* again. Anna Mahler did so and
promptly changed her mind, saying that now she saw the
Tchaikovsky film in a new light. She accordingly granted Russell permission to make his film about Gustav Mahler.

Mahler was originally going to be financed as a British-
German coproduction and was to be shot in Bavaria—until the
German partners "pulled themselves and their money out," as
Russell puts it. "Consequently we shot the movie in the English Lake District and it was all the better for it." The loss of
German financing, however, meant shaving the budget for the
film severely; but Russell, with his wife Shirley's collaboration as costume designer, was once again able to make a low-
budget picture look like a high-budget costume drama, just as
they had so often done in their BBC days.

"I found most of Mahler's clothes in an hour's outing to Car-
naby Street in London," she said at the time that the film was
made. "A black three-piece suit costing about $60 really looks
elegant on film; so does a very good Germanic looking jacket
in cream cotton, and a striped blazer. I've given up sticking
accurately to dates, and now prefer to aim for the right mood
and feeling in the choice of clothes. For example, the extras in
the crowd scenes are all dressed in anything that happened to
be on hand and to fit, from 1870 to 1970. After all, the extras
aren't really noticed very much."

Mahler begins in a beautiful Lake District setting which
serves as the background for the first of the several fantasy
sequences which punctuate the movie. In it Russell visualizes

Robert Powell as Gustav Mahler and Gary Rich, playing the composer as a boy, compare notes on the set of *Mahler* (credit: Ken Russell).

the emotional conflict that developed in Alma as a result of her husband's stifling her musical talent. We see the secluded summer house overlooking a tranquil lake where Mahler spent his summers composing. Suddenly the building ignites into flame, signifying the fire of creative inspiration that rages within him and bursts forth in his music, and which has engulfed his wife's less grandiose musical capacities.

The camera then pans over the lake shore to a bust of Mahler hewn out of granite, and onward to a chrysalis containing a female human form which is struggling to break free from its gossamer wrapping. After giving up the struggle, she apparently submits to remaining so confined, and kisses the bust as a mark of this submission.

That this image is a metaphor for Alma's subservient relationship with her husband is clarified in the dialogue of the scene which follows. Mahler (Robert Powell) awakes from the dream-vision just described and remarks to Alma (Georgina Hale) that while he "slept like a rock" he experienced a dream in which she appeared as a chrysalis struggling to be born. Alma replies sarcastically that she is grateful that he at least pays attention to her in his dreams, and that she is forever overshadowed by him. Irritated, he says that she ought to change her tune; and she responds, "I had plenty of tunes until you killed them all."

The pair are sitting together in the compartment of the train which is carrying them to Vienna, where Mahler intends to rest after collapsing under the excessive demands of his strenuous conducting schedule. Russell employs the train trip as a convenient metaphor for Mahler's journey through life, and therefore structures the film around it: the conversations in which Mahler engages aboard the train with Alma and others precipitate his reveries about the past, which take the form either of straightforward factual flashbacks or of fantasies like the one with which the movie begins, and a somewhat later one which further elucidates the subordinate role that Alma has accepted in her marriage. While Mahler is busy composing his Third Symphony at his lakeside retreat, he sends Alma on an errand to quiet the noises around the countryside which are interfering with his concentration on his pastoral symphony.

Russell exploits the irony of this situation to the full by

showing, in his own words, "Alma Mahler bribing a shepherd to stop piping so that her lord and master will not be disturbed from composing a symphony full of shepherd's piping."[12] As this fantasy sequence continues, Alma silences cow bells and church bells alike, and even buys a round of ale for the village band in the local innyard to distract them from playing for a while, so that she can provide her husband with the atmosphere which he requires to work.

An underlying tone of melancholy suffuses this essentially comic sequence, for Alma's intrepid compliance with her husband's wishes for solitude implies that she is striving to reconcile herself to the stifling of her own musical career by devoting herself in every conceivable way to collaborating with her husband in the creation of his music, even when that collaboration takes the pathetically remote form of merely providing him with the conditions which he demands in order to compose.

Alma's capitulation is made all the more poignant in a later scene in which Mahler patronizes her about a song that she has written by saying that she should leave composition to those who are "too stupid to do anything else." Afterwards Alma ritually buries the manuscript in the woods in a child's pencil box which serves as a small coffin, and with it her hopes for becoming even a minor composer on her own.

Mahler feared that his wife might eventually abandon him for another man in retaliation for the subsidiary position into which she had been forced in their relationship, and Russell formulates this anxiety in still another fantasy sequence. Commenting on the mingling of reality and fantasy in the film, Russell says:

Most of my films on composers evolve through a stream of consciousness in which the man and the myth, the music and its meaning, dream and fact all blend into the mainstream of the film itself. The life span of a man is measured in years, but the screen time of a film about him must be measured in minutes. Given this fact and the nature of the medium, so far as I am concerned, the impressionistic technique works the best. When every second counts, it is often necessary to say two things at once; which is why I frequently introduce symbolism into scenes of reality.

For example, during the last few years of his life Mahler was haunted by the fear that his wife would leave him. When he finally did die, Alma went through three husbands and God knows how many lovers before joining him. So time proved that Mahler's fears were justified. I therefore distilled all the men interested in Alma into one symbolic figure, a man named Max, in the same way that I condensed several of Tchaikovsky's lovers into Chiluvsky in *The Music Lovers*. The nightmare in which Mahler sees his widow desecrating his memory by frolicking with Max on his grave, consequently, helps to establish Max in the film as the symbolic threat to their love.

Russell gives substance to Mahler's anxieties about Max by having Max journeying to Vienna on the same train with Gustav and Alma. Mahler's discovery of Max's presence aboard the train not only fleshes out his fantasy about Max, but sparks a dramatic confrontation between husband and wife in which Gustav gives his wife an ultimatum to choose between himself and her passionate admirer once and for all. She must decide either to get off the train with Max at his station or continue on to Vienna with Mahler. "You've always wanted fame," he snaps: "you may have to settle for notoriety."

Here Russell very astutely integrates Alma's decision about choosing between Max and her husband into the pervasive journey motif of the movie by concretizing it into a choice of detraining with Max or with Gustav; and there is more than a modicum of suspense generated by the scene in which the train pulls into Max's terminal and then pulls out again—minus Max, but with Alma still aboard.

Clearly the complex and delicate relationship of Gustav and Alma represents the main plot of the film, and it is surely strong enough to ground the story of a biopic. If one becomes involved in this key aspect of the plot, then, some of the flashbacks and fantasy sequences not directly related to this central issue of the movie can seem to be mere distractions. One such dream-vision is that surrounding Mahler's conversion from Judaism to Roman Catholicism in order to further his career by ingratiating himself with Cosima Wagner, the anti-Semitic widow of Richard Wagner who will not otherwise allow him to conduct her husband's operas.

"Mahler betrayed himself when he changed his religion ostensibly for social and financial reasons," Russell explains. "In his operas Wagner created a religion of his own based on myth and legend, coupled with anti-Semitism; and this 'religious' claptrap was one of the philosophical foundations on which Hitler's Nazi Germany was built." Russell therefore caricatures Mahler's conversion as being not so much to Roman Catholicism as to Wagner's peculiar, pseudoreligious cult of the superman, as served up to him by Cosima Wagner (Antonia Ellis), dressed up like a storm trooper in drag.

Mahler begins the sequence clad in the black suit and wide-brimmed hat of a rabbi to denote his Jewishness; but the sequence ends with him sporting the knightly costume of the great Wagnerian hero Siegfried. Similarly, the Star of David which he clasped while garbed as a rabbi is transformed in a fiery forge, first into a Christian cross, and finally into Siegfried's sword, which Gustav then presents in tribute to Cosima. In return he is showered with gold coins, a symbolic reminder of the commercial considerations which to some extent motivated his conversion.

Although in general I find the dream-visions in the movie to be inventive and to blend with the overall texture of the film, this particular fantasy seems intrusive because of the comic-strip quality of its design. Such a scene would not be out of place in Russell's *Strauss* film, because Russell fashioned *The Dance of the Seven Veils* from start to finish with the broad strokes of a cartoonist. The bravura style typical of the *Strauss* film, however, jars the more serious tone which Russell has established in *Mahler*. The Cosima Wagner sequence is in sharp contrast not only with the straight narrative episodes in the present film, but also with the more soberly mounted dream-visions in the rest of the film already described.

While it is true that the Cosima Wagner sequence strikes a false chord in the film, however, Stephen Farber goes much too far when he dismisses *Mahler* as a grab bag of flashbacks and fantasies that interrupt the flow of the plot line like the production numbers in an old Hollywood musical.[13] By and large all of the flashback and fantasy sequences flow directly into the mainstream of the movie's narrative continuity, which is solidly structured around the journey motif. The use of the train trip as the frame of reference for Mahler's recollections of his journey through life, furthermore, comes to an appropriate conclusion when Gustav and Alma reach their journey's end in Vienna.

Mahler reaffirms his love for Alma by attesting anew that his music expresses his love for her, and that as long as his music will last their love will also last. "The ending of the film out-Hollywoods Hollywood," Russell comments, explaining that he designed it as a satire on the happy endings of Hollywood biographical movies of the past. In the latter motion pictures everything always worked out for the best, whereas the ending of *Mahler* is happy only on the most superficial level; for Russell overshadows the Mahlers' reconciliation with a reminder that Mahler is, after all, a deathly ill man.

A physician is waiting for Mahler on the platform with the news that the results of an earlier medical examination have proved negative and that Mahler should proceed immediately to a hospital. Mahler cavalierly brushes the doctor aside, but death cannot be long ignored by a fatally ill man. In this context, Mahler's final remarks to his wife are tinged with a darker hue than he is prepared to admit: his prediction that his music will outlast his life will come true sooner than he thinks.

Even though *Mahler* is not the disjointed work that some critics have called it, there is no question that the movie is uneven in quality. Some of the movie's imaginative set pieces, like the pastoral fantasy linked with the composition of the Third Symphony, are right on target; while some others, like the Cosima Wagner segment, misfire.

All in all, however, *Mahler* is a good film and deserved the award for technical achievement which it earned at the Cannes Film Festival. It is a typically eye-filling Russell movie that presents yet another artist who never quite reaches the heroic stature which Russell searches for in the historical figures whom he delineates on film. Up to this point in Russell's career Henri Gaudier came closest to embodying Russell's ideal hero. But it is Rudolph Valentino, as Russell envisions him in his biopic about the silent screen star, who most closely approximates Russell's concept of an ideal hero.

5

The End of the Search: *Valentino*

TO SAY THAT Rudolph Valentino best embodies Russell's idea of a hero is not to imply that Valentino was genuinely heroic in every aspect of his life and character, but that the real-life Valentino provided Russell with the raw material out of which he could fashion a cinematic hero that approximated his concept of greatness without distorting the latter's life and character in the bargain.

Gaudier's early death precluded him from realizing fully the potential greatness that was his; and even though Valentino also died relatively young, he nevertheless had met enough challenges in life to emerge bloody but unbowed from life's conflicts before his untimely death at thirty-one. But like Gaudier he still died before he tarnished his youthful idealism with the compromises of age. This cannot be said of Tchaikovsky, Grandier, and Mahler, or for that matter of Delius, Debussy, Richard Strauss, and Russell's other biopic subjects (cf. chapter two). All of these figures made compromises in their lives and in their art in ways that Valentino did not.

It may seem somewhat incongruous to compare a superstar of the primitive silent screen to composers and practitioners of other art forms which are all more exalted and sophisticated than silent movies ever were. But Russell's point seems to be that a man achieves greatness by living up to his personal code of behavior regardless of the circumstances in which he finds himself. Valentino's code of honor was that which he had brought with him to America from his native Italy. It seemed shopworn and old-fashioned to the progressive modern Americans with whom he came into contact both professionally and personally during the balance of his short life. But as

131

Russell has drawn him in the film, Valentino was willing both to live and to die for that code.

I do not wish to canonize Valentino as Russell presents him in the film, but simply to say that Valentino comes closer to being a genuine hero than any of his predecessors in the Russell gallery. Russell, it is true, emphasized Valentino's good points over his weaknesses of character in the screenplay in a way that does make Valentino more sympathetic and estimable than any other Russell hero; but he has by no means whitewashed Valentino in the manner customary in the old Hollywood screen biographies. Yet Valentino, as he emerges in Russell's movie about him, is a man of character who might well serve as the norm by which to judge the conduct and lives of Russell's previous biopic heroes.

The start of the Valentino project was solemnized one July night in 1975 when Russell gave a dinner party which was attended by Mardek Martin, who was to contribute to the script, and by Philip Jenkinson, a film historian who showed newsreels about Valentino and clips from his films. In the course of the evening Russell several times flipped through a stack of photographs of male actors that were being suggested for the film's title role, including such Italo-Americans as Al Pacino and Robert De Niro. He finally set them aside and said that he was really not concerned about having an actor of Italian descent or a Valentino look-alike play the role. "If you create the proper atmosphere around the actor, it will be believable," he explained, adding that his final choice was probably going to be another Rudolph: Rudolf Nureyev.

Negotiations between Russell and the expatriate Russian ballet dancer had been going on intermittently for years about a proposed film of the life of another Russian ballet dancer, Vaslav Nijinksy. Russell had interested producer Harry Saltzman in the project back in the mid-Sixties, but Nureyev's other commitments always got in the way. Moreover, Nureyev was not particularly impressed with the Russell TV biopics which he had seen, including the one about Isadora Duncan, whom Nureyev thought was more spiritual and less flamboyant a dancer than Russell had pictured her (cf. chapter two). Nureyev's reaction to Russell's subsequent feature biopics, however, was more favorable; and he accordingly warmed to the idea of working with Russell.

On his part, Russell began negotiations with Nureyev over the *Valentino* film by first asking him to play the cameo role of Nijinsky, whom Valentino always insisted he had taught to tango during their early days in New York City. When Nureyev indicated his willingness to play the cameo role, it occurred to Russell that he might also be interested in playing the leading part. "There is no reason why a dancer shouldn't be good in a dramatic role," Russell reasoned, "since dancing means communicating meaning without words—which is just what Valentino did as a silent film actor. Besides, Valentino was a ballroom dancer before he was an actor, and always moved like a dancer on the screen."

As a matter of fact, Nureyev had considered undertaking to play the role of Valentino on the screen when he was offered the part by Vittorio De Sica years earlier. So the thought of enacting Valentino in a motion picture was not new to him. After reading the script, Nureyev decided definitely to do the movie.

By August 1976 the Valentino company had started shooting in Almeria in Spain, and then moved on to Elstree Studios on the outskirts of London. Principal photography was finished, after what Russell calls "twenty-one weeks of concentrated anxiety," in January 1977. "We had originally planned to make the film in Hollywood and I went out there to set things up. But the decision to shoot the movie at Elstree instead was made when we realized that 80 percent of the picture was to be shot on interior sets. Production costs are almost double in the States what they are in England, and so there seemed to be little point in doing the film there at all; and United Artists would not have agreed to the higher budget needed to shoot in Hollywood anyway."

Russell and Nureyev worked with a mutual respect for each other's talents throughout the shooting period, though they never really became friendly. Nureyev approved of the director's custom of recording important scenes on videotape so that the actors could have an instant replay of a given take in order to improve their handling of the scene on the next take. "He's very flexible as a director," Nureyev said during production. "He guides rather than imposes."[1]

When shooting a picture the director always has to be ready for the unexpected; and there is no better example of this

maxim in Russell's career than the set of circumstances that
issued in Russell's playing a cameo role in *Valentino*, that of
Rex Ingram, the director of Valentino's first major movie, *The
Four Horsemen of the Apocalypse*. An actor had originally
been engaged for the role, which required that he stand on a
six-foot observation platform overlooking a battlefield set and
shout directions at the extras through a megaphone. The actor
in question suffered from vertigo and could not do the scene.
So Russell took megaphone in hand and replaced him. Russell
thought no more about the incident until he returned to London to find that the irate actor had taken up the matter with
Actors Equity. "They said we'd have to go back to Spain and
reshoot the scene," Russell recalls, "because I wasn't in the
actors union. We in turn pointed out that the actor had appeared on the set fortified with liquid courage to do the scene
and dressed inappropriately as a cowboy. Equity dropped the
matter."[2]

The Rex Ingram incident marked the only time that Russell
has essayed a speaking part in one of his films, but he has
made several fleeting appearances in his movies throughout
the years. The alert filmgoer can see him surface briefly as a
passerby whom Amelia bumps into on the street while looking
for a new pair of angel wings in his early short film; as Isadora
Duncan's irresponsible chauffeur who carelessly throws her
precious love letters to the winds in *Isadora*, and as the crippled Captain Patterson who rescues Isadora from one of her
suicide attempts at the seaside; as the randy village curate
whom the devout Eric Fenby is disedified to find snuggling
up to a parishioner in a back pew in *Delius*; and as an invalid
in a wheelchair among Tommy's fans in the "Come to This
House" number in *Tommy*. But whether Russell makes a
token appearance in one of his films or not, his signature as the
director who oversees every aspect of the production from
script to scoring is evident anyway.

When *Valentino* was ready for scoring Russell said in a letter, "Music plays as big a part in *Valentino* as if I were making
a movie on a composer. We have used a lot of music by Ferde
Grofé of Grand Canyon Suite fame. I discovered that he had
also written a dozen and a half other compositions, many of
which had intriguing titles such as World's Fair Suite and Mis-
sissippi Suite. He died about fifteen years ago; but I met his

son when I was in Los Angeles and he placed at my disposal old tapes and discs of Forties broadcasts, etc.—with the result that I realized that Grofé's type of tuneful, rather dated and idiosyncratic style would well suit our slightly satirical film."[3]

The satirical elements in *Valentino* are directed primarily at the exploitation of Valentino by Hollywood in order to sell his movies and by the press to sell newspapers. The public image of Valentino the superstar of the silent cinema is contrasted throughout the film with the private image of the unhappy man that Valentino really was in his personal life.

"In my view," says Russell, "his story is about a man who wore a mask in public and was quite different in private. In working out the script we explored Valentino's sexual life and the rumors of his homosexuality more than any other screen treatment of his life has done, including both the 1951 motion picture with Anthony Dexter and the 1975 TV movie with Franco Nero. Valentino's first marriage lasted only one night; the big question is why, and the only person who could answer it was eighty years old when we made the picture and would not see anyone. But I was not really concerned about separating the man from the myth because it's impossible to sort them out. And with my penchant for mixing reality and fantasy in my film biographies, I really was not inclined to do so anyway.

"The film treats his second marriage to Natasha Rambova in great detail, and then moves on to his final downhill plunge to death. As I see it, Valentino died to save his honor, not his pride; and since the idea of someone sacrificing himself to satisfy his honor seems right and inevitable to me, that is the way I present it in the film."

Russell judges the screenplay of *Valentino* to be the best that he has ever worked on, and there is every indication that he is right. The carefully structured script begins with a prologue set during Valentino's wake, which serves as the frame of reference for the whole film in the same way that the train trip provided narrative continuity for *Mahler*. As each mourner enters the funeral parlor and recalls that period of the deceased actor's life in which they knew him most intimately, flashbacks portray for the viewer the events that are recalled.

The prologue really begins during the credits, which are superimposed on authentic newsreel footage of what at first looks like a crowd of fans mobbing a Valentino premiere, but turns out to be his mourners rioting outside the funeral parlor while his wake is being held inside. By way of making a smooth transition from the newsreel material to the reenactment of the wake in the film's opening scene, black-and-white shots of Richard Rowland, MGM's chief executive (Alfred Marks), frantically handing out admittance passes into the funeral parlor are skillfully intercut with the actual newsreel shots of the mobbing fans.

Then the camera takes us inside with Rowland, where Valentino is shown lying in state in an elaborate coffin surrounded by the chiefs of the studios where he had worked. All three men are preoccupied with the loss of Valentino, not as a person but as an investment. Suddenly the hysterical mob breaks through the funeral parlor windows and into the room where Valentino's corpse is being exhibited. After the riot is quelled, reporters comb through the knots of people milling around the casket for individuals who knew Valentino; and one journalist spots Bianca de Saulles, Valentino's first love after his arrival in America. He shrewdly bargains for an interview with Bianca in exchange for not tipping off his colleagues to her identity.

More than one American critic singled out these opening scenes of the film, with the greedy movie moguls and opportunistic journalists, as setting what they considered to be the anti-American and anti-Hollywood tone of the picture. Richard Schickel in *Time* excoriated Russell for his "relentless anti-Americanism, implying that the unfortunate inhabitants of these shores are the only citizens of the world capable of materialism or vulgarity."[4]

On the contrary, Russell, like any satirist, is exposing the faults of our flawed human nature—which happen to be manifest in this case in Americans in general and in the denizens of Hollywood in particular, since Hollywood, USA, is where Valentino lived and worked. In contrast to those who manipulated Valentino for their personal aggrandizement are others—also Americans and Hollywoodites—who showed him kindness, notably June Mathis (Felicity Kendal). June Mathis not only is instrumental in the course of the film in furthering Valentino's career in pictures, but also bails him out of jail anonymously with her own money when he is imprisoned for alleged bigamy.

Russell believes that *Valentino* is not anti-Hollywood, much less anti-American. "I don't hate Hollywood," he insists. "I am passionately dispassionate in my treatment of it in *Valentino*. Some studio executives like Jesse Lasky were hard on Valentino, so I show them being hard on him. Anyway, there is no point in hating Hollywood; that would be like hating the sphinx: it's just there, and it will go on being there whether you like it or not."

In any event, the prologue of the film closes with the reporter meeting Bianca, and the picture proper begins with her recollections of her brief interlude with Valentino. She remembers walking into the ballroom where Valentino was engaged as a taxi dancer and watching him give a tango lesson to Nijinksy. Afterward, while Valentino is dancing with her, Bianca's irate husband storms across the dance floor to berate his wife for two-timing him with a "powder puff dago" who has been observed dancing with another man.

Nijinsky (Anthony Dowell) learns to tango from Valentino
(credit: United Artists).

Valentino looks to the manageress of the ballroom for support, not realizing that it is she who phoned de Saulles, with whom she is having an affair, to give him the upper hand over his wife. This is only the first of many female betrayals of Valentino, so naive where women are concerned, that we will witness in the film. Bianca at least appreciates him, and is truely touched by his gallant offer to marry her and to assume responsibility for her little son as well, although things eventually do not work out that way.

June Mathis is also impressed by Valentino from the very first time that she sets eyes on him, as an exhibition dancer in a cabaret. As June watches Valentino tango, he is photographed from overhead through a row of light bulbs strung across the ceiling, which symbolize the lights of the movie marquees which will soon enshrine his name.

Because she is an important screen writer at Metro, June is able to wangle Valentino a small but meaty role in *The Four Horsemen of the Apocalypse*, in which he tangos his way to almost instant fame. After she makes him a star, Valentino is taken up by the renowned actress Alla Nazimova (Leslie Caron) to play opposite her in *Camille*. He then falls under the influence of Nazimova's protégée, Natasha Rambova, née Winifred Hudnut, the stepdaughter of a wealthy cosmetics manufacturer who has become a set and costume designer (Michelle Phillips).

In his films Russell has often examined a problem that is endemic to all artists, regardless of their particular field of artistic endeavor: the conflict of illusion and reality in the artist's life. Because an artist devotes himself to manufacturing illusions for others, he runs the decided risk of confusing the world of illusion with which he is constantly involved with the real world in which he lives. This problem surfaces often in the present film, but is particularly evident in terms of Valentino's relationship with Natasha.

Although his screen image is that of an overwhelmingly strong-willed male, Valentino can be easily dominated by the women in his private life. Valentino seems unaware that Natasha has gradually managed to subjugate him not only in their personal relationship but by taking charge of his career as well. Perhaps because he has begun to believe in his own screen image, he refuses to believe that she has such a strong hold on him.

Russell illustrates the painful gap between reality and illusion in this instance by building a scene in which Natasha proves her power over Valentino. At the end of a day of shooting on *The Shiek*, Natasha entices Valentino into the shiek's tent on the set, where she coyly arouses his ardor and then coolly refuses his embraces. Her purpose is to play "hard to get" until she has manipulated him into promising to divorce his estranged first wife and marry her, and also to allow her to have the final say on the choice of all of his future film projects. Valentino submits to her wishes on both counts, refusing to admit even to himself how totally she has vanquished him.

This portrayal of Natasha's conquest of Valentino the man is followed immediately by a scene from *The Shiek* in which Valentino the actor ravishes a helplessly passive female with all of the fiery passion and determination that was so conspicuously lacking in his foregoing real-life encounter with Natasha.

But Valentino is not alone in his inability to sort out fantasy and fact in his life. As June Mathis watches this seduction scene unreel on a movie screen, she tearfully fantasizes that it is she that is being crushed in the strong arms of the shiek. The implication is that no one in tinsel town, even the no-nonsense June Mathis, is completely free from this syndrome of mixing reality and illusion.

The Mathis sequence just described represents the only serious failure in narrative logic in the entire movie. The recollections in this part of the film are being narrated by Natasha Rambova; hence June Mathis's private fantasies about Valentino simply have no place in a flashback presented from Natasha's point of view. But this exception proves the rule that by and large Russell is careful to derive exposition in a given flashback only from the person whose memories are being depicted for the viewer at that point in the movie. Moreover, Russell slips this lapse of narrative logic by the viewer so adroitly that hardly anyone who sees the film notices it.

There is another sequence in the picture which caused a severe critical reaction, however. It is the one in which Valentino is forced to spend the night in a California jail as an alleged bigamist because California law does not recognize his divorce from his first wife as final and thus rejects his marriage to Natasha. Jesse Lasky, boss of the studio where Valentino works, refuses to put up bail because of the free publicity at-

Valentino with Natasha (Michelle Phillips) in re-creations of two classic films: dancing in *The Four Horsemen of the Apocalypse*

romancing in *The Sheik*.

tending the star's temporary incarceration. And so Valentino is thrown into the drunk tank for the night, where he is taunted and humiliated by prisoners and guards alike. He even suffers the supreme indignity of urinating in his pants when his bathroom privileges are revoked because he refuses to display "the eighth wonder of the world" for all present.

In discussing *Mahler* Russell made the point that, because screen time is so short, it is often necessary to say two things at once in a scene, "which is why I frequently introduce symbolism into scenes of reality." In the jail sequence Russell was indeed saying two things at once. First of all, he wished to comment on the callousness of a studio executive who would allow his biggest star to languish in a jail cell for the sake of free publicity. Secondly, the director wanted to use the scene to depict the enormous hostility which Valentino had unwittingly evoked in the American male population, which had become increasingly jealous of the sexual prowess which he exhibited on the screen. Russell thus distills the animosity of American men across the nation toward Valentino into this scene in which the jailer and the prisoners get their chance to demean "the shiek" in the name of all the men everywhere who have been made to feel sexually inadequate in the face of Valentino's virile screen image.

Because Russell wanted to make both of the points mentioned above in this single sequence, the scene starts realistically enough, but then escalates into a sordid nightmare of male mockery being heaped upon the common rival of them all. It is a matter of record that such male antipathy toward Valentino did exist, and that it culminated in a snide editorial in the *Chicago Tribune* which charged Valentino with being both impotent and homosexual, and as such unworthy to represent genuine manhood on the screen.

Valentino retaliated with an open letter which denounced the editorial for slurring his family name and Italian ancestry by casting doubts upon his manhood. Furthermore he challenged the anonymous author of the editorial to a boxing match as a test of honor. His challenge went unacknowledged by anyone at the *Tribune*; but Frank O'Neil, the boxing writer for the *New York Evening Journal*, offered to take Valentino on in a private sparring match. At the end of the bout O'Neil was surprised to find himself flat on the mat. After picking himself up, he good-naturedly admitted to having a new respect for Valentino, who had proved that he was no powder puff.

As an object lesson in Russell's method of cutting across the biographical facts of a person's life to create a dramatic sequence in a biopic, it is well worth noting that he has dramatized the incidents surrounding this episode in Valentino's life into a spectacular manner which goes beyond the known facts in many details, but which nonetheless is faithful to the facts in essence.

In the movie Valentino's challenge to the *Tribune* is picked up by Rory O'Neil, a belligerent, contemptuous sports writer who also happens to be a retired navy boxing champion. His bout with Valentino is staged, not in private, but in an arena filled with wealthy socialites in evening dress, some of whom even waltz around ringside between rounds. Obviously the contest which means the vindication of his honor to Valentino is but a frolic to the onlookers.

At first the ex-champ gets the better of his novice opponent and the crowd cruelly tosses pink powder puffs into the boxing ring, paralleling the way that spectators at a bullfight hurl pillows into the bullring to jeer at an unsuccessful bullfighter. But Rory O'Neil is both drunk and out of shape, and finally caves in under Valentino's fervent onslaught.

Valentino bests O'Neil again later in the evening by proving that he can outdrink as well as outbox him, and Valentino staggers home, weary but triumphant. But the strenuous exertions of the night have taken their toll on the already critically ailing man, and he slumps to the floor of his living room just as he reaches for an orange from the bowl on the table. As he dies, his unsteady hand grasps for the orange, which remains tantalizingly out of reach, just as his dreams of retiring someday to the seclusion of a farm to raise oranges has likewise eluded his grasp to the end.

Russell has mounted the prize fight so elaborately in the film in order to make it serve as an important metaphor for man's struggles in the contest of life. Valentino takes a lot of punishment in the battle of life, just as he does in the boxing ring; but he always goes down swinging and is the ultimate victor according to the standards of his venerable code of honor. Consequently, though the match which Valentino fought in real life was in private, the director had reason to

orchestrate it in the grand manner which he employed in the
motion picture to underline its importance to Valentino's personal honor and to his public image.

As Alexander Bland puts it, the big set pieces in the film,
such as the prison scene and the prize fight, fall naturally into
place within the framework of the movie as a whole because
they are plausible. They are in each case founded on facts
which are magnified but not distorted in the film. In the
screenplay Russell "zooms in on a few incidents and expands
them to produce the maximum effect," Bland concludes.
"Russell has taken liberties; but he has not strayed into
license."[5] A basis can be found in any standard biography of
Valentino for the general outline of events that are covered in
Russell's screenplay; but he has allowed his creative imagination free reign, as he always has, in filling out the details of
each episode for the screen.

In the film Valentino sees the boxing and drinking bouts as
the twentieth-century equivalents of a traditional duel,
whereby he can establish once and for all his masculinity and
thus prove that he is no effeminate weakling offscreen who is
unworthy to represent genuine masculinity onscreen. In making this point in the movie, however, Russell does not *ipso
facto* resolve the questions surrounding Valentino's private
life and personality. Russell implies but does not say for certain that Valentino was a latent homosexual whose sexual am-
biguity caused the breakup of his unconsummated first marriage and left him prone to the domination of overbearing
women like Natasha Rambova.

But what Russell does insist upon in his concept of Valentino is that this man was a professional artist devoted to his
work, who transcended the personal problems of his private
life to become one of the first legendary actors of the screen.
In Russell's view, what makes a great artist is the ability to
transcend one's personal inadequacies in practicing one's art;
what makes a great man is the ability to transcend one's personal drawbacks in living one's life in harmony with one's
principles. The Valentino who emerges from Russell's film
gets high marks in both categories. Whether or not the critics
were prepared to accept this larger-than-life, heroic portrait of
Valentino, few denied that this is the way that Russell meant to
draw Valentino in the film. Even Richard Schickel, who dis-

liked the film, speaks of Valentino's "saintly patience and stoic courage" as reflected in the movie.

Anwer Bati in *Punch* went much further and defended the director and his film against the charges of those critics who felt that the movie misrepresents Valentino's life. "I must say that I find it amazing that critics still treat Russell's 'biographical' films as if they were *supposed* to be definitive, carefully researched screen representations of the lives of his subjects," Bati wrote; "it just isn't what he sets out to do." What Russell does set out to do, according to Bati, is to offer his audience "a series of vivid cinematic dreams about his subjects," which nevertheless illuminate the facts of those subjects' lives. In this case Russell explores the psychological problems of a matinee idol whose private life is dominated by women to the point where his virility is publicly questioned.[6]

That Russell's delineation of Valentino in his film is not at all far removed from the real-life Valentino is clear from the opening description of Valentino in Robert Oberfirst's biography, which is significantly subtitled, *The Man behind the Myth*: "Because he was an American screen idol most people tend to forget that he was foreign to the ways of America. His outlook on life was that of a better-than-middle-class Italian brought up in a home filled with sentimentality and close family ties. Honor was a principle to die for; love of family and ancestry was a principle to live for."[7]

This then is the man and the artist who seems best to embody Russell's notion of a hero: someone who has more good qualities than bad and who uses the former to transcend the latter, not only to realize his artistic talent but also to mature as a human being. In creating a full-length portrait of a man and artist of this stature, Russell has in the bargain made a movie that will in time be recognized as one of his richest and warmest motion picture.

In the three musicals which we will consider in the next chapter we shall continue to find traces of the same themes about the artist and his life which have preoccupied Russell in his biopics: Polly in *The Boy Friend* must choose between a private life and a public career; and the hero of *Tommy* and the Liszt of *Lisztomania* are by turns idolized and then rejected by a capricious public in much the same manner as Valentino was. Given Russell's persistent themes, then, one can be no

more than momentarily surprised that Russell's musicals reflect the same preoccupation with the conflict of illusion and
reality in the lives of artists which one finds in his biopics.

These musical films are hardly marginal to Russell's career,
therefore, for he wrote the screenplays for all three and
lavished his inexhaustible fund of visual imagery on their
musical numbers. Indeed, this trio of musicals can tell us almost as much about Russell the filmmaker as his biopics can;
and one of them, *Lisztomania*, in many ways is a biopic.

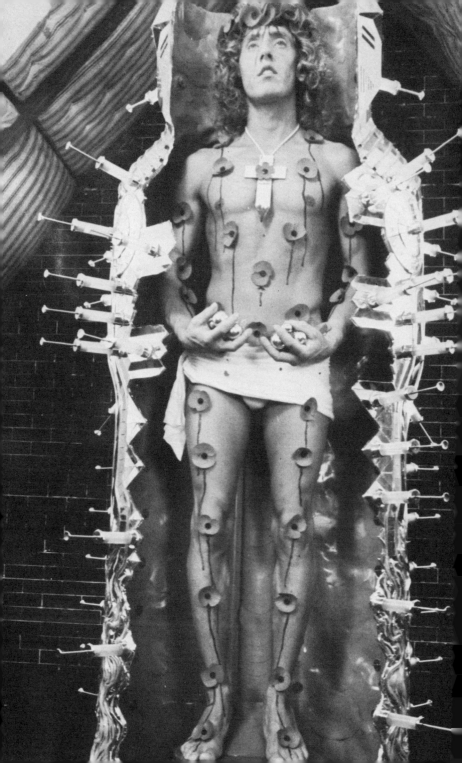

6

More Music Lovers: The Musical Films

COLIN WILSON has said that Russell's unrealized projects reveal a great deal about his proclivities as a filmmaker, and it is worthwhile to survey these unmade films briefly before going on to his trio of musicals, especially since Russell cribbed bits from his unfilmed scripts for some of the production numbers in his musicals.

After finishing *Savage Messiah* in 1972, Russell decided to use George Neveux's dream play *Juliette* as the springboard for his next film. Neveux's drama recounts the search of a young man for the girl who will incarnate his dream of the ideal woman; but Russell's screenplay shifted the emphasis of the original play from the female pursued to that of the male pursuer. Russell's script evolved into a modern parable about the temptation of the artist in the materialistic modern world to compromise his artistic integrity for commercial gain. The framework in which this theme, so fundamental to Russell's biopics, is illuminated in the script is the journey of a young filmmaker, Michael Mann, to an Eastern European film festival. Two episodes in the script are especially noteworthy because of their incorporation by Russell in a revised form into later screenplays, as we shall see later in the chapter.

The first of these revolves around Poppy Day, Mann's most important superstar, whose presumed death prompts her disconsolate fans to erect a shrine in her honor, to which invalids are brought in the hope of cures. But Poppy's spurious death, it turns out, was all part of a cruel publicity stunt which reaches its climax when Poppy herself descends from a helicopter that is hovering over her shrine. The pilgrims are understandably enraged when they discover the cynical way in which they have been manipulated, and a riot breaks out.

149

ger Daltrey as the suffering hero in Tommy 1975)
edit: Columbia).

The other important incident in *The Angels* which Russell was to salvage for later use is that of Mann's filming a TV commercial for baked beans, obviously founded on Russell's own unpleasant recollections of his interim assignments directing television commercials. A child actor is to register supreme delight over the plate of beans he is gleefully consuming. The beans, however, are served cold because steam would fog the camera lens; then they are sprayed with a plastic cellulose so that they will shine under the lights on the set. The boy scoops up a mouthful of what is supposed to be a delectable dish, swallows, smiles contentedly—and promptly throws up the indigestible mess. To Russell this brief scene epitomizes the phoniness that is inextricably bound up with commercialized art, of which making TV commercials constitutes the nadir, since they represent the ultimate prostitution of the artist's talent.

Russell feels very strongly on this point, and firmly believes that the ad men are shaping society according to their own empty values. To illustrate his point, he recalls an example of false advertising to which he now regrets having been an accomplice: a soap manufacturer purported to merchandise a detergent whose suds quickly drained away, when in fact the suds actually clogged the drain of the sink.

In order to make the soap suds appear to behave as advertised, Russell had to photograph the suds being pumped up through the drain and into the sink, and then run the film backwards to give the impression that they were disappearing down the drain just as quickly as the manufacturer boasted that they would. For Russell that commercial was the last straw. When he thought about the technical skill that was being employed for these dishonest purposes, he was sickened by the prospect of doing any more commercials.

Financing was not forthcoming for *The Angels*, so Russell used the script as the basis of another screenplay entitled *Music, Music, Music,* about John Fairfax, a serious composer who is reduced to writing jingles for TV ads. Russell again used the baked-beans commercial sequence from *The Angels*, but this time ended it with the child who has just vomited the baked beans leaving the studio with John, who composed the score for the commercial, to get a breath of fresh air. Once outside, John is hit by a car and knocked unconscious; he then fantasizes about the commercial compromises of composers throughout the history of music, including Liszt, Wagner, and others.

The upshot of this excursion into the past is that John awakes to resolve that he will abandon not only the writing of TV jingles but even the composition of his religious rock opera, tentatively entitled *Jesus on Venus*. Instead he decides to compose a choral work for children's chorus which will reaffirm the indomitability of the human spirit, an oratorio centered on the theme of death and resurrection.

Russell, however, continued to be dissatisfied with the script, and wrote in a letter in the fall of 1972, "I have wrestled with my new *Music* script unceasingly and have at last emerged—the loser! It just won't work out. It's all too downbeat and morbid. I've written and re-written the damned thing about four times, and spent the best part of six wasted months on it. It started as *Juliette*, metamorphised into a couple of versions of *The Angels*, went on to *Music, Music, Music,* and ended up as *Come the Revolution*. What I had intended to be a history of music has turned out to be a catalogue of betrayal, compromise, and disillusionment. All of the composers I dealt with, including Bach, Beethoven, and Prokofiev, began with great aspirations and ended up selling out in the end. I had intended it to be a more personal and optimistic kind of film."[1]

A third film which Russell prepared at this time that also went unproduced was an Italian coproduction of Rabelais's *Gargantua*, as much a satirical jibe at the establishment as *Angels* and *Music* had been, but this time conceived in a more farcical vein and, therefore, more optimistic and positive in tone.

Two episodes from *Gargantua* would find a place in subsequent Russell films. The first parodies a religious communion service, performed by the citizens of a totalitarian state: a patrolman-priest consecrates a bottle of Coca-Cola, using the hood of a car as an altar; he then smashes the bottle over the head of one of the communicants, while others are served their communion repast of Cokes and hamburgers. The other incident in *Gargantua* that Russell would utilize in a later film shows the giant Gargantua experiencing an erection so enormous that it becomes an impromptu maypole which his companions merrily festoon with flowers and then dance around.

This elaborate production proved too expensive to mount, so Russell set this script aside also, to await the day when it, along with his other abandoned projects, would provide a storehouse of untapped material for his two rock films, *Tommy* and *Lisztomania*. But before Russell made these two musicals, he filmed *The Boy Friend* as his first excursion into the realm of movie musicals.

The Boy Friend (1971)

The Boy Friend marked a complete change of pace for Russell from the biopics which he had been doing up to that point. It was a screen version of Sandy Wilson's musical toast to the Twenties. Even this film, however, is something of a departure from established ways of movie making. Russell was out to prove that a lush-looking musical can be made for $2 million—$20 million less than was spent on *Hello, Dolly!* "After the strain of making a violent film like *The Devils*," says Russell, "I thought I would try making a musical film just for fun. But *The Boy Friend* turned out to be the most complicated project that I had ever attempted, given the time and money I had to work with."

Helping him to give *The Boy Friend* a lavish look was, as in the past, his wife and costume designer, Shirley, whose talent for transforming clothes that she buys in a bargain basement in the morning into costumes that look radiant on the movie set later that same day has always been something akin to magic.

When I visited the set of *The Boy Friend*, Russell, inexplicably clad in a sailor suit that was a couple of sizes too small for him, was directing a musical number that was designed to be a homage to the Busby Berkeley extravaganzas of the Thirties. A group of girls were arranged in geometric patterns on a giant phonograph record, as technicians scurried around out of camera range.

At the end of the day's shooting, Russell recounted how his script for *The Boy Friend* had evolved. "When I was preparing my screen version," he said, "I heard that an amateur dramatic society was putting on the show in Chingford, Essex; and I decided that it would be useful to go along and see it. The cast got wind that I was there and played it up to the hilt. Meanwhile, I was sitting there in the audience watching the show, mentally visualizing how I was going to stage the musical numbers on film."

Later he got hold of a 16mm film of the original 1954 British production of the show with Julie Andrews, which had been made to assist the New York company during rehearsal. "It was funny and touching at first, with everyone striking poses," he recalls; "but as the film went on, one got bored with the cardboard characters in a way that one didn't when watching them on the stage. That's when I realized that I would have to do the original musical as a show-within-a-show if I were going to sustain the audience's interest throughout the film. I remembered the amateur production that I had seen in Essex and how the performers had played their parts to impress the visiting film director, and decided to frame the original show within the context of a backstage musical of the sort that Hollywood turned out in the Thirties, with the cast all competing for the attention of the visiting film maker who has come to see the performance." The opening credits of the film set the tone of an early Thirties Hollywood backstage musical by announcing, "Ken Russell's Talking Picture of *The Boy Friend*."

Polly, the heroine of the film (Twiggy), is the understudy of the leading lady in a tacky stock company which is putting on *The Boy Friend*. When the star of the company (Glenda Jackson in a cameo appearance) breaks her leg, the director of the troupe pushes Polly onto the stage as her replacement with Warner Baxter's line from the Berkeley 1932 musical *Forty-Second Street*, "You're going out there as a chorus girl, but you're coming back a star!" The rest of the cast is jealous of Polly, and tries to sabotage her performance. Furthermore, Cecil B. de Thrill, a Hollywood director interested in making a movie of the show, is present at the performance, and all of the performers try to upstage each other as well as Polly, in an effort to gain his attention. The production numbers in the film are projections of how de Thrill imagines that he would stage some of the songs in a lavish Hollywood film.

"I tried to get the extravagant, imaginative flair of the Busby Berkeley musicals into these production numbers," Russell explained; "but it was difficult to accomplish in a British studio, where they had forgotten how to do an old-fashioned musical. Of course they've done things like *Oliver!*, where you build naturalistic sets and have the chorus dance around them.

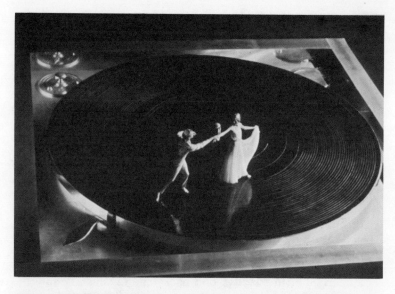

The Boy Friend: Twiggy and Christopher Gable in tributes to famous makers of musical comedies – Busby Berkeley (top) and Astaire and Rogers (bottom).

The chorus in another Berkeley-type number (top) and with Tommy Tune (bottom) (credits: M-G-M).

But I am referring to the kind of musical number which involves a lot of special effects and camera tricks. Take the song
in *The Boy Friend* called 'There's Safety in Numbers.' By
means of optical effects the chorines seem to spin into pin-
wheels, and then turn into dancing dominoes. That took some
doing because I was shooting with a British crew who had
never done this sort of thing. Everything was late in being
built, didn't work, or fell over."

Despite the handicaps under which Russell was shooting
his ambitious production numbers, his fabled temper never
flared once during the time I observed the shooting—though
just about everyone else's did. When the cinematographer had
a dust-up with the camera operator, Russell arbitrated the dis-
agreement. "Now what we have here is an artistic difference,"
he said consolingly. Russell then proceeded to indicate to the
camera operator precisely how he could maneuver the camera
around the set in order to get the angle for the shot which the
director and the cinematographer wanted. "Actually it was a
technical problem and not an artistic one," Russell commented as he resumed his place in the director's chair next to
the camera. "But technicians like to be thought of as artists;
and they are."

Besides his tribute to Busby Berkeley's musicals in *The Boy
Friend*, Russell also designed a production number as a homage to the Astaire-Rogers musicals, in which a group of dancers cavort on the glittering wings of a vintage biplane as it
swoops through a snowstorm, recalling the finale of the
Astaire-Rogers musical *Flying Down to Rio*. As the number
ends in Russell's version, the sumptuous set conceived by de
Thrill in his imagination dissolves to the flimsy painted flat
that must serve to suggest an airplane on the tawdry stage on
which Polly and her companions are performing the number.

In this way Russell suggests here as elsewhere in the film
the theme of the contrast between illusion and reality which
he had explored more fully in several of his biopics. Polly, the
naive understudy getting her first taste of the theater, is constantly surprised by the difference between the way her fellow performers look backstage (so grotesque in their heavy
stage makeup) and the way they look onstage (all glowing and
radiant before the footlights). Even the has-been soprano who

gargles with gin in the wings takes on an aura of elegance when she makes her grand entrance onstage.

The Boy Friend succeeds, then, because the frame story which Russell has provided for the film gives the original stage musical an added dimension on the screen which enhances the whole movie. In the context of the frame story, for instance, Polly is an inexperienced understudy, and this makes the viewer accept Twiggy's limited talents as a singer and dancer as the disarming charm of a newcomer, because that is what she is supposed to be in the plot of the film.

In the end de Thrill decides to scrap the idea of filming *The Boy Friend* in favor of doing *Singin' in the Rain* instead; but he offers Polly a contract. So Polly must decide whether or not she wants to make a career of bringing a little magic into the drab lives of the townspeople where the troupe is situated, or whether she wants to accept de Thrill's offer of a Hollywood contract. But she turns down the opportunity to become part of the Hollywood dream factory in favor of staying on in the company and falling in love with the company's male lead (Christopher Gable). Unlike Tchaikovsky and the central characters of other Russell biographical films, Polly is not a romantic idealist who pretends to be more than she is. Hence one finds in *The Boy Friend* resonances of the illusion / reality theme which Russell has treated more seriously in other films, but no more sincerely than here. It is clear, then, that Russell's great variety of movies — although superficially quite different — have after all sprung from the same creative consciousness.

Yet no element in a Russell film is so precious to him as writer or director that he cannot reexamine it with a cold critical eye in order to reassess whether or not it contributes to the total effect of the film. "I'm not adverse to making something better," he says. "Some of my colleagues found one of the production numbers in *The Boy Friend* overlong and rather out of tune with the rest of the film, and I also thought that the film played better without it. So that was one of the things which I cut when the studio asked me to trim the film from 128 minutes to an even two hours."

Russell has always nursed a cordial dislike for *The Boy Friend*, and it is only relatively recently that he has had any-

thing good to say about it. This is probably because of the
great technical difficulties which he encountered in shooting
the film's complex production numbers, and because he bat-
tled with MGM for months over making additional cuts in the
movie for distribution in the United States. The front office in
Hollywood feared that American audiences would not appreciate some of the musical segments in the picture that af-
fectionately recall old-time British music-hall acts. Compromises were reached, but Russell continued to refer to the
movie as "the butchered *Boy Friend*," especially when it was
shorn even more drastically to fit into a ninety-minute slot for
prime-time TV in America.

Still, when he was preparing to shoot *Tommy* three years
later, he remarked, "I heard the complete musical sound track
of *The Boy Friend* the other day. At least it was original and
inventive—largely thanks to Peter Maxwell Davies's witty
scoring."[2] Maxwell Davies's arrangements are a delight, but
Russell deserves more credit for his mounting of the film than
he is prepared to grant himself. The visual creativity mirrored
in the musical numbers of *The Boy Friend* is that of Ken Russell. In fact only the artist who conceived the lavish production numbers of *The Boy Friend* could have taken on the formidable task of bringing *Tommy* to the screen.

Tommy (1975)

Although Russell reached back to earlier unfilmed scripts
for imagery that could be integrated into his screenplay of
Tommy, this does not mean that *Tommy* is a mere grab bag of
remnants that Russell pieced together by simply ransacking
his shelved scripts. On the contrary, the material which Russell incorporated into *Tommy* from his earlier efforts served to
stoke the fires of his imagination into creating other imagery
for the film.

"*Tommy* is loaded with material from previous scripts," he
says. "Variations of the baked beans sequence in *Tommy* were
in *The Angels* and in *Music, Music, Music*, while a variation on
the shrine sequence in *Tommy* turned up earlier in *The Angels*
and in *Gargantua*. I don't know what I would do without my
rejected scripts."[3]

When Russell agreed to adapt *Tommy* to the screen, he faced the formidable challenge of staging a seemingly endless series of musical numbers for the film version because the original rock opera on which the movie is based is really a succession of songs with no spoken dialogue whatever. *Tommy*'s first incarnation was in a record album as a rock opera composed by and for the English rock group The Who. The album proved so popular that The Who began performing it in a concert version onstage, with Pete Townshend, its principal composer, and the other members of The Who adding to the score and revising it from time to time.

Producer Robert Stigwood purchased the screen rights at this point, and asked Russell to listen to the album with a view to doing the film. Russell, an inveterate aficionado of classical music, found *Tommy* unfamiliar, even unpleasant to the ear the first time he heard the score. But when he met Pete Townshend, who elaborated the philosophy on which the work was based, Russell became intrigued with the venture and got to work on it in earnest.

"The imaginative scenes which are meant to visualize the songs in the film were stimulating for me to do because in them I was exploring the interior world of the characters, particularly of Tommy himself," says Russell.

It was much harder to formulate images on the screen for the symphonic music in my biopics about composers like Mahler and Tchaikovsky than it was to create visual metaphors for music that had lyrics as well, as in the score of *Tommy*. Creating images to accompany symphonic music really stretches the imagination because one has to think of images that not only serve as counterparts to the music, but which lead into other images as well. In working out the visuals for each successive musical number in *Tommy*, I was forced to think of images that commented on the lyrics of the song in question, but which also expanded its meaning, and helped to develop character as well. I didn't just want to illustrate the songs on the screen, as if I were merely giving a slide lecture about the rock opera. The latter approach simply amounts to trading on the composer's hard work and contributing nothing of your own as a filmmaker. My task was to get the maximum amount of emotional feeling into a minimum number of images for each song.

Tommy, as a film based on a rock opera, is highly imaginative throughout—until the ending when Tommy's fans rebel; and then I employ a more realistic treatment as they destroy the national resort-shrine built in his honor, after they discover that his mother and stepfather have been using it for commercial exploitation of them. One is prone to fall back on clichés in scenes of straight reportage of this sort. The best sequences in *Tommy*, I think, are the ones in which reality and fantasy mingle, as when I project for the viewer Tommy's hallucinations while he is on a drug trip.

But even in the scenes primarily preoccupied with the plot line of the rock opera Russell has made significant changes and additions whereby he has strengthened both the story and the characterization. As he puts it:

I found that I had to fill in gaps in the story that went unnoticed when one listened to the recording of the show or saw *Tommy* done in a concert version on stage. I felt that one shouldn't lose track of important characters as the story unfolded. While Tommy is busy becoming Pinball Champion of the World, for example, his mother drops out of sight in the original story. I told Pete Townshend that we needed a number showing her enjoying the luxuries which Tommy's success has brought her. He replied that he had toyed with the idea for a number called "Champagne," and I said that that would be fine. I also thought that audiences could only identify with the people on the screen if they knew something about them. So I added the prologue, which I believed was essential to establish Tommy's background and the kind of people that his parents and his stepfather were.

The prologue of the film is done entirely in pantomime. It is set in 1945 and begins with Tommy's father, Group-Captain Walker (Robert Powell), standing on a hillside and contemplating an incandescent sunset, and then rejoining his wife, Nora (Ann-Margret), nearby at their hushed lakeside retreat. They make love, for it is the night before Walker must return to his squadron and go off to die in an air battle. It also proves to be the night of Tommy's conception.

One night sometime later, Nora senses that her husband has been shot down because his picture falls to the floor during an air raid. The shattered glass of the picture frame suggests to her the shattered glass of her husband's cockpit windshield as it is riddled with enemy shrapnel. We see that her worst fears are well founded as Russell cut to Walker crashdiving to earth. Tommy's father is reported missing in action before Tommy's birth, and so Nora experiences both joy and pain as the fatherless baby is born on the day that the war ends. And with that, the prologue comes to an end.

By the time Tommy is six years old, Nora has taken a lover named Frank (Oliver Reed). They are making love in Nora's bed one night while Tommy lies sleeping in his own room. Suddenly the scarred face of his father, only recently cured of amnesia, is looking benignly down on the sleeping boy. Tommy wakes up just as the shadowy figure of his father is leaving his bedroom, so he rises to follow him down the corridor and into Nora's room. Tommy stands traumatized in the doorway as Frank ruthlessly crushes Capt. Walker's skull with a heavy lamp. With that, the man so recently returned from the dead perishes for good.

Nora and Frank shout at Tommy that he has seen and heard nothing—not realizing as yet that the boy has been struck deaf, dumb, and blind by this experience, which has caused him to withdraw into a private world of his own. The light bulb that flickered and went out in the lamp that Frank used to murder Tommy's father betokens the extinguishing of Capt. Walker's life, and also implies that Tommy is now dead to the terrifying external world outside of him.

In the prologue and opening scenes of *Tommy* just described Russell has created a gem of visual storytelling that distills an enormous amount of exposition into a few moments of screen time that remain indelibly impressed on the filmgoer's memory not only throughout the balance of the movie, but for a long time afterward. The shift from the idyllic love relationship of Tommy's father and mother to the sordid lust and violence that disfigures her affair with Frank is perfectly accomplished; the prologue furthermore establishes the pattern of the whole movie which shifts back and forth from the point of view of the gentle Tommy, who is so like his dead father, to that of the callous Nora, brutalized by her relationship with Frank.

The transition from Tommy the boy (Barry Winch) to Tommy the man (Roger Daltrey) is accomplished with the same visual economy that has characterized the movie from the beginning: a close-up of little Tommy staring blindly into the distance dissolves to a close-up of the grown-up Tommy wearing the same blank expression on his face.

Tommy's guilty mother has heeded his oft-repeated plea (which is heard on the sound track as a projection of his inner thoughts) to "see me, feel me, touch me, heal me," by bringing him to the shrine of Marilyn Monroe, goddess of the silver

Tommy: (top) the young Tommy (Barry Winch) and his mother (Ann-Margret); (bottom), Ken Russell directing the shrine sequence.

(Top), Oliver Reed as the wicked stepfather; (bottom), Tommy (Roger Daltrey) delivers his message of salvation (credits: Columbia).

screen, in the hope of a cure for her deaf, dumb, and blind son. In images that Russell developed from the similar shrine sequences in the unfilmed *The Angels* and *Gargantua*, the director pictures cripples paying homage to their idol while a larger-than-life statue of Marilyn is carried aloft over their heads in a procession down the center aisle of her basilica amid puffs of incense and hymn-singing. The faithful then partake of the communion service in which they receive seconal and Johnny Walker Red in place of the traditional consecrated bread and wine of an authentic sacramental Mass (paralleling the Cokes and hamburgers that the communicants in the script of *Gargantua* receive from their "minister").

After the mob of worshipers have dispersed, Nora leads Tommy up to the gigantic plaster effigy of Marilyn that she fervently hopes will restore him to the world of the senses. But just as Tommy's fingers make contact with the base of the statue, it topples to the marble floor and smashes to pieces. This scene was criticized as antireligious in some quarters, harkening back to similar accusations against *The Devils*. But Russell's intent was far from blasphemous or sacrilegious, and he explains why:

The scene in which her faithful followers come to worship at the shrine of the dead superstar is not a criticism of religion, but of the way that fans can deify superstars whom they idolize, whether they be movie idols or rock idols. The last shot in the scene is of the statue of Monroe crashing into rubble. My point is that no human being can live up to the idealized image of them which their fans build up for them, and the latter are therefore doomed to disillusionment. Through no fault of his, Tommy becomes such an idol and ultimately repudiates this kind of adulation, though his mother and stepfather exploit his fans for all they are worth. The Monroe scene foreshadows the disillusionment of Tommy's fans later in the film with the heroic image which they have created of him, and which they demand that he live up to.

After Nora fails to cure Tommy's catatonic state by means of her pseudoreligious superstitions, Frank decides to jolt the young man into reentry of the real world by an injection of LSD administered by the Acid Queen (Tina Turner). This sequence turns out to be one of the most stunning phantasmagorias that Russell has ever conceived. "When the Acid

Queen injects Tommy with drugs," Russell comments, "I tried to project onto the screen the experience which Tommy is having in such a way as to indicate that his acid trip triggers memories of his past life as well as causes him to hallucinate."

In preparation for his fantastic journey, Tommy is shut up in a chromium-plated "iron maiden" covered over with drug-injecting syringes whose needles sink into his flesh and launch Tommy on his fantasy flight (see the illustration at the head of this chapter). In the course of this extended dream vision, the iron maiden opens to reveal Tommy's father inside instead of Tommy, evoking how desperately Tommy misses his father and identifies with him so closely. It opens once again and this time Tommy has materialized as St. Sebastian, the Christian martyr of ancient Rome who was executed with arrows. In Tommy's drugged vision of himself at this point, then, the Acid Queen's hypodermic needles have been symbolically transmogrified into the arrows that killed St. Sebastian. Each wound on Tommy's body is covered with a red poppy, the flower that is traditionally placed on the graves of dead soldiers in England on Remembrance Day, and which once more recalls the cherished memory of Tommy's father. At this point Tommy evokes not only the martyrdom of St. Sebastian but also the death of Christ on the cross, since his bloody body is covered only with a loincloth, as was Christ's body when he was crucified, and his bleeding head is crowned with poppies that suggest Christ's crown of thorns. Tommy's incarnation as Christ is a premonition of his later becoming a kind of messiah for his fans, and ultimately suffering for his efforts to lead them to a more exacting kind of existence (see chapter head).

When the iron maiden opens for the last time, Tommy's acid trip is over and he falls senseless to the floor. But he awakes to find himself no different than he was before. Drugs are not the answer to Tommy's deaf, dumb, and blind state, any more than the Monroe shrine was. Even after Tommy becomes the pinball champion of the world, he still remains in his continuing solipsistic trance. Nora accordingly feels more guilty than ever about her son because his catatonia precludes his enjoying the luxurious fruits of his success as she does. The more opulently she dresses, the more cosmetics she applies, the more haggard and wretched she really looks. (Little wonder that Ann-Margret received an Oscar nomination for effecting this transformation in herself, in her performance as well as in her appearance.)

After watching Tommy win his most crucial match on TV, Nora drunkenly smashes the picture tube of the set with an empty champagne bottle and then deliriously imagines that all of the products which she has just seen advertised on television are flooding into her living room like lava erupting from a volcano. Harkening back to the baked-bean, chocolate, and soap commercials that Russell had made in his early days in TV, and to his burlesquing of them in the scripts of *The Angels* and *Music, Music, Music*, he shows billowing cascades of baked beans, chocolate pudding, and soap suds bursting through the TV set and completely innudating her. As she wallows in the mess like a true devotee of the consumer society, she presses a bouquet of white flowers to her cheek and soils them in the process. Nora is a ruined woman who tarnishes everything she touches, one infers; and this is why she is unworthy to reach the insulated Tommy, though she continually tries to do so.

As she watches Tommy staring blankly into a mirror, she flies into a frenzy of despair and hurls him through the mirror, just as she earlier threw the champagne bottle through the picture tube. But this time it is Tommy and not Nora who has the fantastic experience. Like Alice in Wonderland, Tommy is catapulted through the looking-glass and lands in a new world, the realm of the senses: Tommy can see, hear, and speak once more.

The hordes that followed Tommy's rise as pinball champion now come to him as pilgrims seeking to share the cleaner, more noble kind of existence to which he calls them at his camp in the mountains. But Nora and Frank turn the whole operation into a money-making venture. The adoring crowd of pilgrims one day turns into an angry mob as they express their resentment at the exorbitant prices of the Tommy souvenir T-shirts, LP's, etc.; but more importantly they are angry because they have not achieved the instant inner peace which Tommy enjoys. They begin to riot and finally burn down the camp and murder Frank and Nora, leaving Tommy all alone once more.

After Tommy's ordeal by fire, he plunges into a lake to be cleansed and reborn. In the film's finale he ascends the mountainside like a latter-day Moses to contemplate the sun-set—just as his father did at the beginning of the movie. His identification with his father has apparently brought him closer to his Father in heaven, to whom his last exultant song seems to be addressed. Stephen Farber would press the religious symbolism of the movie's ending further still. "The film is cyclical in structure, beginning in innocence and ending in innocence reclaimed," he writes. "The ending is meant to echo the crucifixion and the resurrection."

In *Tommy*, Russell again attacks the cheap commercialization and trivialization of religion, as he did when he focused on the souvenir-sellers in his short film on Lourdes and the carnival atmosphere of the public exorcism in *The Devils*. But, as in these earlier films, he ends *Tommy* on a note of spiritual affirmation which clearly endorses the spiritual values of the messianic, Christlike Tommy.

Russell makes Tommy a heroic figure, but Tommy does not qualify as Russell's most imposing hero in the way that Valentino does, for the simple reason that Tommy, as the central character in a parable, is just too good to be true. As Farber puts it, Tommy's "plastic purity" looks wan by comparison with other, more human Russell heroes.[4]

Lisztomania (1975)

In *Lisztomania* Russell presents Franz Liszt as the first superstar composer, and thus combines the rock-opera format of *Tommy* with the biography of a composer which recalls his other biopics. This blending of two genres in which Russell has worked before is epitomized by the songs in the film, which consists of Liszt's melodies set to lyrics by rock composer Rick Wakeman. And because *Lisztomania* is a combination of two genres with which Russell has been associated, it is a fitting film with which to end this study.

It would be pleasant to be able to record that *Lisztomania* succeeds both as rock movie and as biopic, but unfortunately that is not the case—as Russell is the first to admit.

"I got off on the wrong foot with *Lisztomania*," he concedes, "even though it starred Roger Daltrey, who played Tommy. It called for a bigger budget than we had, and so the film doesn't work as well as I wanted it to. The symbolism, moreover, is a

Roger Daltrey before the credits in *Lisztomania* (credit: Movie Star News).

bit too relentless and the fantasy sequences tend to submerge the reality of the characters. I think I had exhausted the vein of biographies of composers at the time I made *Lisztomania*, at least for a while."

Indeed, the film is painfully derivative of his earlier films, particularly in his employment again of Nazi symbolism recruited from both his Strauss and Mahler films. "I'm going to lay off the swastikas for a while," he says. Nevertheless, *Lisztomania* is worth discussing because of his experiment in the blending of genres and because no Russell film, after all, is ever without interesting elements and imaginative touches, regardless of one's overall assessment of a given film; and *Lisztomania* is no exception to this rule. When Russell fails, he fails as stylishly and grandly as he succeeds at other times.

Russell raps Franz Liszt in the film for trading his artistic aspirations for commercial emoluments, in the same comic-strip style that he utilized to criticize Richard Strauss for the same thing in *Dance of the Seven Veils* (cf. chapter two); but the Strauss film is fresher and funnier than the Liszt film. Nevertheless there are some fine cinematic touches in *Lisztomania*, and one of them is the precredit sequence. Liszt is caught by an aging nobleman *in flagrante delicto* with Marie, the man's youthful wife; and the scene is rife with humorous sexual puns. While the betrayed husband duels with the interloper, a chorus on the sound track comments that the fighting is as furious as "balls of fire"; and with that the count thrusts a burning candelabrum between Liszt's legs. When the countess complains that her love for her elderly husband has long since been extinguished by his impotence, the candle in her own hand wilts. And so on.

Russell designed the duel sequence to recall anyone of several similar scenes in the old Douglas Fairbanks and Ronald Colman swashbucklers, and the film as a whole is filled with similar references to other movie genres. In the ensuing fantasy sequence the count boxes Liszt and Marie inside a grand piano, and then orders it tied to a railroad track—thus reviving one's memories of the old silent serials. An onrushing train plows into the piano with a blinding crash, which leads into the credits and on to one of the best scenes in the movie, a typical concert during one of Liszt's many enormously successful tours.

Russell, who believes that Liszt's popularity made him the first superstar, stages the recital like a rock concert. As Richard Schickel succinctly sums up the event, Liszt "tries to satisfy the demands of his groupies (they want him to play his hit, 'Chopsticks'), his conscience (by introducing some new music by a radical named Richard Wagner), and his id (by casing the audience for a suitable post-concert bed partner)." Schickel—never one of Russell's great admirers—believes that the analogy between Liszt and a modern rock star is a point well taken; but, he adds, "Analogy . . . is not drama. Whatever point *Lisztomania* has to make is nailed down in one scene."[5]

On the contrary, Russell's depiction of Liszt in the concert sequence as trading on his talent for easy success by pandering to his fans is the premise of the entire movie, and it will take the balance of the film to explore it.

Throughout the picture Russell shows Liszt consistently falling short of his own aspirations, both as a man and as a composer. Liszt's failure in both spheres of his existence is further examined in the scene in which he decides to give up serious composition in favor of going on yet another lucrative concert tour, and to leave Marie and their three illegitimate children behind in order to be free of marital responsibilities while he carouses through Europe. That Liszt has aspirations to a higher kind of life is projected in a fantasy sequence modeled on a similar dream sequence in Chaplin's silent classic *The Gold Rush*.

Accompanied by his own Liebestraum (Dream of Love), Liszt, who is made up to look like Chaplin's celebrated Tramp, is enjoying his own "dream of love" with Marie in a log cabin filled with heart-shaped pillows which bespeak the deep-seated love which characterized the early days of their relationship. Liszt looks wistfully at a blank page of sheet music and truly regrets having to interrupt his serious composing to go off on a concert tour; but as he munches on a crust of stale bread, he realizes that he must do so if he is to support his impoverished family, whom he would not think of leaving behind.

As all four members of the Liszt family joyfully set out on their journey together, they are photographed through the open cabin door as they recede into the distance; and the cabin door closing behind them functions like an iris-out in a silent film, blacking out the screen.

This reverie serves as a painful reminder to Liszt of how his attitude toward his composing and his family has deteriorated over the years. The gap between the way Liszt is and the way he would like to be, however, closes as the movie goes on; and that is the axis on which the plot turns. But Liszt will get worse before he gets better; and this is clearly indicated by his affair with Carolyn, a Russian princess, while he is on tour. This episode precipitates the daffiest, most outrageous fantasy sequence that Russell has ever concocted.

As Liszt and Carolyn make love, he literally disappears into her giant vagina and is catapulted into a lair filled with all of his former mistresses. Liszt serenades this bevy of females with the music of his Orpheus Tone Poem, and like an Orpheus tries to soothe their hostile feelings toward him with his music; but they will not be so easily mollified. Taking a leaf from his *Gargantua* script, Russell has Liszt sprout a ten-foot penis which the ladies duly mount as if it were a cannon and do a tap dance on it. Then they stand it in a perpendicular position and festoon it with flowers and ribbons as if it were a maypole and play ring-around-the-rosie.

Finally they lower the penis into a horizontal position once more and guide it toward a guillotine. As Liszt fruitlessly begs the women to spare his precious member, Carolyn explains that they are going to liberate him from his slavery to the flesh so that he can write the great music which he is capable of composing. As the blade falls, Liszt wakens abruptly from his reverie just as a piano lid bangs down on his—thumb.

Liszt has been jolted by this dream vision in a significant way; for this fantasy, weird as it is, serves as a turning point in the film. For the first time he realizes that he is growing weary of the wild life which he has been leading; and he decides first to begin composing once more, and ultimately, to become a cleric.

At this point Richard Wagner (Paul Nicholas) enters his life again, and Russell dramatizes Wagner's cribbing bits from Liszt's music for his own compositions by showing Wagner drugging Liszt and then, Draculalike, burying his fangs in Liszt's neck while the latter is slumped over the piano.

Wagner thus drains off some of Liszt's musical inspiration for his own use.

Wagner is transformed by turns from being Dracula into Dr. Frankenstein, and later into Frankenstein's monster. As Dr. Frankenstein he shows Liszt the giant superman which he is perfecting in his laboratory and which he will glorify in his music in order to unite the German people into a strong nation of warriors, a master race such as they were in the days of the legendary Siegfried. He has already begun to organize a youth corps led by his wife, Cosima, Liszt's daughter. The youngsters are all dressed in uniforms modeled on that of the cartoon character Superman.

Liszt is determined to thwart Wagner's maniacal plans and seizes upon the idea of exorcising Wagner's demoniac inclinations with the power of his own music. He rushes to the piano and tears into a fast and furious rendition of his own Dance of Death, which sets the piano into a spin and causes it to sprout flamethrowers which set Wagner's castle afire and bring the whole edifice down on top of him.

After Liszt's own death later in the film, he looks down from heaven to find that Wagner has risen from his grave as a monstrous robot with the face of Adolph Hitler and is wreaking destruction and havoc everywhere with a machine gun shaped like a guitar. Liszt climbs into the cockpit of a space ship fashioned from organ pipes and flies down to earth to destroy the berserk Frankenstein's monster, which has become a hideous parody of the glorious superman which Wagner had envisioned. Liszt machine guns the Hitleresque monster, symbolic of the fascist dimension of Wagner's music, and flies back to heaven, singing joyously that the world has attained peace at last.

Liszt himself had already achieved peace in his later life by renouncing his frivolous ways and devoting his mature years to his art. Portraying this gradual development in Liszt's character, however, was beyond the meager acting abilities of Roger Daltrey. Daltrey was perfectly acceptable as Tommy because he was really not called upon to act very much at all in playing what was in essence a one-dimensional role, only to sing. Even the relatively simple characterization of Liszt in Russell's script exceeded his capabilities as an actor. By contrast, Paul Nicholas ably handles himself in all of the various transformations that Wagner undergoes in the course of the picture, from budding composer at the beginning to robot at the end.

The real problem with *Lisztomania* is not Daltrey's performance, however, but that there is simply too much fantasy and not enough fact in the screenplay. As Russell himself confesses, "The fantasy sequences tend to submerge the reality of the characters." Unlike his other biopics in which fantasy sequences figure, Russell does not provide the audience with sufficient background material on the historical personages in order for them to grasp the significance of the dream visions in the film.

The residue of biographical material that underlies the screenplay is fair enough to both Liszt and Wagner as far as it goes. Liszt was a notorious womanizer who sired several illegitimate children and ended his days as a cleric. In addition, music scholars confirm that Wagner did borrow from Liszt's innovative musical style and adapt it to his own compositions; and Hitler himself affirmed that Wagner's revival in his operas of the legendary pagan heroes of German mythology helped to buttress the ideology on which the Third Reich was erected.

But Russell seems to suggest that none of Wagner's music possessed any goal but a political one; and that is an oversimplification of some magnitude. Still, in fairness to Russell, it must be noted that the Nazi fantasy sequences in *Lisztomania* are not meant to be taken literally; they rather express, as Stephen Farber astutely points out in the essay mentioned above, Russell's fears about what can happen when art is perverted by show business and by political fanaticism. The fact that the majority of Russell's biopics portray the artist's betrayal of his vocation does not obscure his belief in the moral importance and the influence of art.

Ultimately Russell has tried to cover too much ground in *Lisztomania*, ranging from Liszt's youth to beyond his death, and encompassing so much material about Wagner along the way that one begins to wonder which of the two composers the movie is really about; and the fact that Nicholas's performance consistently overshadows Daltrey's tends to obscure Liszt's central place in the picture even more.

At one point in the film Liszt remarks that time in the end kills critics, while art lives on. But the critics at the time of

Lisztomania: (top) Roger Daltrey as the devilish composer, Franz Liszt; (bottom) Ringo Starr as the Pope surprises Liszt in his boudoir. "The fantasy sequences submerge the reality."

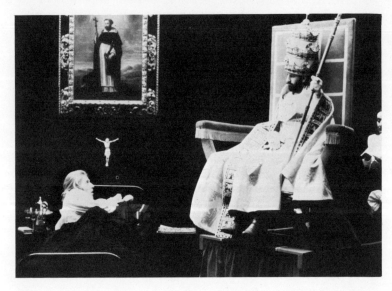

Lisztomania's release were very much alive and very vociferous. Peter Davis subtitled his angry piece in the *New York Times* "Brilliance Gone Berserk," and went on to say that Russell's method of embroidering the basic historical facts which he uses as the basis of a biopic has become "more idiosyncratic and stylized with each successive movie," and that *Lisztomania* was the most unreal and nightmarish of them all.[6]

Davis is right in his assessment of *Lisztomania*, but he is wrong in trying to construct an artificial continuity in Russell's biopics, whereby they have become increasingly more fantastic and phantasmagoric from picture to picture. The Strauss TV film, done five years earlier, belongs to the same fantasy-filled comic strip genre as *Lisztomania*. By the same token, Davis is wrong when he contends that Russell never again achieved the kind of muted subtlety that marked his 1968 *Delius* film, since *Savage Messiah* (1972) is cut from the same cloth as *Delius*.

There is no denying that all of Russell's biopics reflect his personal reaction to the subjects, as Russell himself insists. He treats each of his subjects as they strike him, sometimes creating caricatures done in primary colors, sometimes painting their portraits with soft pastels. Hence the series of Russell biopics simply will not fit into the neat pattern into which Davis has sought to force them.

The one thing that all of the biopics do have in common is Russell's persistent conviction that the artist must maintain his artistic integrity inviolate against the threat of crass commercial compromise if he is to produce works of lasting value. Once the artist becomes governed solely by the principles of the marketplace, he cheapens his art and its potential impact, as Russell has illustrated over and over again in his biopics about Tchaikovsky, Mahler, and others.

A quality common to all of Russell's films, biopics or not, is the incomparable visual style which marks every film. The carefully worked out visual symbolism of the Chaplinesque fantasy in *Lisztomania*, for instance, touchingly evokes domestic bliss, while the Orpheus sequence bawdily reflects Liszt's seemingly insatiable sexual appetite. Both of these sequences, though totally different in tone, testify to Russell's unsurpassed visual flair.

Russell is obviously more at home in the realm of the image

than in the realm of the word; the corollary to this proposition is that creating dialogue and narrative structure is not his strong suit. Consequently, the scripts on which he has had a collaborator or which are based firmly on a preexisting work such as a play or a novel tend to be better constructed than those which he has written completely on his own. The visual logic of his fantasy sequences in *Lisztomania* is impeccable, but the narrative logic of his screenplay is at times hard to follow. Important elements of Liszt's life, such as the legal and canonical obstacles involved in his attempt to marry Princess Carolyn and his corresponding decision to take orders in the Church instead, are tossed off in snatches of dialogue before the viewer has a chance to grasp their import.

In the final analysis, *Lisztomania* fails because Russell tried to accomplish too much within the framework of a single motion picture. He had already made a successful rock opera and several good biopics about classical composers, but his effort to mix the oil and water of these two very different genres into a single movie just did not work out. Ross Care sums up *Lisztomania* in *Film Quarterly* as a movie that is caught in a limbo between the kind of movie that would appeal to devotees of classical music on the one hand, and the kind that would appeal to rock fans on the other. Consequently, it is left "sadly dangling, a brilliant, unique, and intensely personal film in search of an audience which perhaps doesn't even exist."[7]

Russell cannot be faulted for experimenting in his films, however, just because the experiments do not all succeed. A movie maker who does not take risks in creating his films will surely fall by the wayside, whereas a venturesome director whose reach sometimes exceeds his grasp continues to be of interest. Critics and audiences alike too often are impatient with an artist's need to ripen and develop his talent gradually; a serious artist needs and deserves some degree of tolerance and patience on the part of critics and audiences while he refines his methods and style. In the upcoming epilogue, then, I shall make some concluding remarks about how Russell and his work have progressed up to this point in his career.

7

Epilogue

IN THE TWO DECADES which have encompassed Russell's career so far, he has almost singlehandedly revolutionized the whole concept of the conventional film biography – to the point where that genre will never be quite the same again. One need only watch a heavily romanticized Hollywood biography like *Night and Day*, ostensibly based on the life of Cole Porter, to grasp how Russell's biopics have come to grips with the problems of an artist's life in relation to his work in a way that makes for a much more challenging and entertaining film than this sugar-coated kind of screen biography does. There was as much night as day in Porter's life, but one would never know it from watching the 1946 film which purports to be his life story.

In addition to experimenting with the nature of biographical films, Russell has at the same time been seeking by trial and error to discover in all of his films, biopics or not, to what extent a motion picture can be cut loose from the moorings of conventional storytelling. If these experiments in narrative technique account for the occasional lapses in the narrative logic of a Russell film, they also account for the intricate and arresting blend of past and present, fact and fantasy, in his best films. The provocative and fascinating body of work that Russell has created so far already assures him a place in the history of world cinema.

One of Russell's admirers is Dick Bush, who has served as cinematographer on several Russell films, including the 1978 TV biopic *Clouds of Glory* (cf. chapter two). Bush says that he finds working with Russell more rewarding than working with almost any other director. "I think Ken gets more out of me than any other director," he explains. "He gives you a chance

179

to do things your way before he makes suggestions, and so he brings out the best in you. That also means that he demands a lot, but the end product also gives you more satisfaction. He pushes the people he works with, but he pushes himself just as hard. We had a terrific row after *Tommy*, and I swore that I would never work for him again. Then I was asked to give some presentations at the National Film School; and I showed *Savage Messiah*, which I think is one of his most sensitive works, and some of the other films we worked on together. I began to realize how much I owed to him; and later, when I was asked to photograph *Clouds of Glory*, I was delighted."

Clouds of Glory was the last Russell film for which Shirley Russell designed the costumes. Since then the Russells have decided to go their separate ways, both professionally and personally. Shirley has gone on to design costumes for, among other films, John Schlesinger's *Yanks*. "I am glad she is pressing on without me," Russell comments. For his part, Russell turned his thoughts to several possible projects; these included an adaptation of *Dracula*, for which he would go back to the original novel as his principal source, and not to any of the previous film or stage versions. "It is really a very Catholic story," he points out, "with those interlocking Catholic themes of sin, forgiveness, and redemption that my films have always been concerned with." His next film, however, was a science fiction thriller based on Paddy Chayevsky's novel *Altered States*.

Although Russell has often been looked upon as a maverick who makes films that are perhaps more subjective and personal than many of the other directors working today, it is important to realize that his motion pictures have been financed and distributed by some of the oldest and biggest of the Hollywood studios: United Artists, MGM, and Warner Brothers. That these companies have been willing to allow him such a great degree of artistic freedom is yet another indication that the big Hollywood studios are well aware that they must make an effort to present contemporary audiences with fresh material and not just a rehash of the old commercial formulas that have long since become overfamiliar to moviegoers.

On the other hand, a canny director like Russell, as independent as he is by nature, realizes that a filmmaker must cooperate with the studio that has invested in his film if he expects to get backing in the future. In other words, the cooperation must be on both sides; and Russell does not mind meeting company demands as long as he can meet them in his own way. "I now have it stipulated in each of my contracts," he says, "that any film of mine must run for three weeks in its initial engagement in the edited version which I have approved and that any cuts that are made subsequently before further release are made under my supervision."

As television more and more becomes the medium which claims the largest segment of the mass audience in the way that the cinema once did, motion pictures are being thought of more and more in the same category as the legitimate theater: a medium that can afford to appeal to the more discriminating audience that wants fare that is a bit more challenging than what they can usually find on the tube. As this happens, film directors like Ken Russell are being given a freer hand in making films that are ever more inventive and personal than has been the case in the past.

After all, the major studios began to extend artistic freedom to independent filmmakers in the first place because studio executives realized that they were losing touch with the moviegoing public's taste. The great virtue which Russell and directors like him have in common is that they have for the most part been able to make films their own way, while at the same time being aware of what will appeal to their audience. The best proof of Russell's box-office pull is that he is the only British director in history ever to have three films playing first-run engagements in London at the same time: *The Music Lovers*, *The Devils*, and *The Boy Friend*.

Commenting on this, Russell says, "I want to entertain people rather than ram ideas down their throats. I follow this code: entertain first, instruct second. I've got lots of films inside me. Some of them will be good, some will be bad. But I'll go on, whatever the critics say about me."

Twenty years ago, when he was first starting out as a filmmaker, Russell described how each potential film takes shape in his imagination: "The images in my mind are all perfectly exposed, there are no scratches, nothing is out of focus, the actors are superb and do everything without being told, and the weather conditions are all one could ask for. But, because we are not all telepathic, the film has got to be made," so that he can share it with others.[1]

One Sunday morning in spring recently, Russell and I sat

discussing his career in his cottage in the Lake District where he works on his scripts and sometimes edits a film and which he calls "a veritable cottage industry of film production." The strains of a Delius composition unexpectedly wafted through the room from the radio. The music turned our thoughts from his more recent films back to his earlier TV biopics such as the Delius film. As our conversation thus ranged across his whole career, it occurred to me that Ken Russell has never lost the conviction that he had learned from the short life of Henri Gaudier, which Russell expresses this way:

Everyone is a potential artist who has something in him which he can transmit to his fellows and which might well be of use to them. It is a pity when one, either through force of circumstance or because one is afraid of being ridiculed by others, won't produce and expose to everyone that little spark of something special which is unique to him alone. I am still striving to accomplish this in my work, and will go on doing so—despite the fact that after every film I always say that I'll never make another one. Somehow I always do.

Somehow he always will.

Notes and References

Chapter One

1. Letter to Gene Phillips, July 2, 1976.

Chapter Two

1. Quoted in Joseph A. Gomez, *Ken Russell: The Adapter as Creator* (New York, 1977), p. 46.
2. Quoted in John Baxter, *An Appalling Talent: Ken Russell* (London, 1973), p. 136.
3. *Delius as I Knew Him* (London, 1966), p. 162.
4. Baxter, p. 14.
5. Russell, letters to Gene Phillips, October 30, 1972; April 17, 1975; July 30, 1977.
6. "Ken Russell: Britain's Stormy Film Maker," *Telegraph Sunday Magazine*, July 16, 1978, p. 36.

Chapter Three

1. "Ken Russell's *Billion Dollar Brain*," *Time*, January 5, 1968, p. 74.
2. Quoted in Baxter, p. 169.

Chapter Four

1. (London, 1974), pp. 38-41.
2. "The World of Ken Russell," *Film Quarterly*, 25 (Spring 1972), 14.
3. Quoted in Rex Reed, "Richard Chamberlain" in *People are Crazy Here* (New York, 1975), p. 184.
4. Catherine Drinker Bowen and Barbara von Meck, *Beloved*

Friend: The Story of Tchaikovsky and Nadejda von Meck (New York, 1937), pp. 106-107.

5. "Russellmania," *Film Comment*, 11 (November-December 1975), 41.

6. *Ken Russell* (New York, 1977), p. 128.

7. "Three Masterpieces of Sexuality: *Women in Love, The Music Lovers,* and *The Devils,*" in Thomas R. Atkins, ed., *Ken Russell* (New York, 1976), p. 65.

8. *Collected Essays* (London, 1970), p. 131.

9. Letter to Gene Phillips, December 31, 1971.

10. Quoted in John Baxter, *An Appalling Talent* (London, 1973), p. 196.

11. Quoted in Baxter, p. 223.

12. Letter to Gene Phillips, April 17, 1975.

13. *Film Comment*, 11 (Nov.-Dec. 1975), 41.

Chapter Five

1. Quoted in Alexander Bland, *The Nureyev Valentino: Portrait of a Film* (New York, 1977), p. 58.

2. Letter to Gene Phillips, February 9, 1977.

3. Letter to Gene Phillips, January 9, 1977.

4. "Ken Russell's *Valentino*," *Time*, October 17, 1977, p. 98.

5. Bland, pp. 48-49.

6. "Rudi's Rudolph," *Punch*, October 12, 1977, p. 670.

7. (New York, 1977), p. 4.

Chapter Six

1. Letter to Gene Phillips, October 23, 1972.

2. Letter to Gene Phillips, February 28, 1974.

3. Letter to Gene Phillips, April 17, 1975.

4. "Russellmania," *Film Comment*, 11 (November-December 1975), 44.

5. "Ken Russell's *Lisztomania*," *Time*, October 10, 1975, p. 61.

6. "Ken Russell's Film Studies of Composers," *New York Times*, October 19, 1975, II, 1.

7. "Ken Russell's *Lisztomania*," *Film Quarterly*, 31 (Spring 1978), 61.

Chapter Seven

1. "Ideas for Films," *Film: The Magazine of the Federation of Film Societies*, January-February 1959, p. 15.

Selected Bibliography

1. Books

ATKINS, THOMAS R., ed. *Ken Russell*. New York: Simon and Schuster, 1976. This collection of essays that covers Russell's major TV documentaries and feature films is a well-illustrated introduction to his work since three of its contributors have written books on him.

BAXTER, JOHN. *An Appalling Talent: Ken Russell*. London: Michael Joseph, 1973. Long on interview and background material, though short on commentary, this book is a handy guide to Russell's career up to *Savage Messiah*.

BLAND, ALEXANDER. *The Nureyev Valentino: Portrait of a Film*. New York: Dell, 1977. A behind-the-scenes glimpse of the filming of Russell's *Valentino* which is sumptuously illustrated in color, but which focuses as much on the film's star as on its director.

The Boy Friend: The Return of Entertainment. New York: Souvenir Books, 1971. A useful brochure about the making of the film which profiles the major cast and production staff members as well as the director.

GOMEZ, JOSEPH. *Ken Russell: The Adaptor as Creator*. New York: Pergamon Press, 1977. A thoroughly researched analysis of the TV and feature film-biographies of Russell, emphasizing how he has reshaped his sources according to his own personal vision and style.

Mahler. London: Sackville Publishers, 1974. A souvenir booklet filled with background data on the composer's life and on Russell's screen adaptation of it.

ROSENFELDT, DIANE. *The Film Career of Ken Russell*. Boston: G. K. Hall, 1978. A comprehensive reference guide to Russell's life and work that details all of the research materials available on his career. The introductory critical essay on Russell's work tends to be somewhat glib at times.

185

WILSON, COLIN. *Ken Russell: A Director in Search of a Hero.* London: Intergroup Publishers, 1974. A brief, highly personalized appreciation of Russell's films up to *Savage Messiah*, which also comments on what Russell's unrealized projects reveal about his personal vision.

2. Parts of Books

ARMES, ROY. *A Critical History of British Cinema.* London: Secker and Warburg, 1978, pp. 302-307. Given the survey format of this book, Russell's work is neatly placed in the context of British cinema as a whole.

KAEL, PAULINE. *Deeper into Movies.* New York: Bantam Books, 1974, pp. 174-80, 302-307, 477-82. Although rather apoplectic in tone, Ms. Kael's reviews of *Women in Love, The Music Lovers,* and *The Boy Friend* nevertheless raise crucial artistic questions about Russell's film art.

———. *Reeling.* New York: Warner Books, 1977, pp. 77-85. *Savage Messiah* is treated in much the same acerbic manner as Ms. Kael deals with other Russell films in *Deeper into Movies,* but she asks the right questions about the nature of film biography.

REED, REX. "Ken Russell: On Location" in *People are Crazy Here.* New York: Dell, 1975, pp. 251-56. A somewhat satirical view of Russell shooting *The Boy Friend.*

ROBINSON, ROBERT. "While the Sun Shines" in *Inside Robert Robinson.* London: Penguin Books, 1965, pp. 73-75. This account of one day's location shooting on *French Dressing* by a TV reporter who has a cameo role in the film humorously describes the impact of the film crew on the sleepy seaside town.

THOMAS, LAWRENCE. "Ken Russell's *The Boy Friend*" in *The MGM Years: The Golden Age of Movie Musicals.* New York: Columbia House, 1972, pp. 30-31. A very favorable treatment of the film, situating it in the mainstream of the MGM musical tradition.

TYLER, PARKER. "The Fatal Kinks" in *Screening The Sexes: Homosexuality in the Movies.* New York, 1973, pp. 282-319. This chapter includes a rather flippant account of the homosexual dimension of *Women in Love* and *The Music Lovers.*

WALKER, ALEXANDER. *Double Takes: Notes and Afterthoughts on the Movies, 1956-76,* London: Elm Tree Books, 1977, pp. 63-65, 82-84. Includes reviews of *The Devils* and *Mahler* by the most severe British critic of Russell's work, whose remarks are nonetheless thought-provoking.

———. *Hollywood, UK: The British Film Industry in the Sixties.* New York: Stein and Day, 1974, pp. 387-92. An overview of Russell's work in the context of the British films of the Sixties, which tends to favor his TV work over most of his features except for *Women in Love*.

WHELDON, HUW, ed. *Monitor: An Anthology*. London: MacDonald, 1962. Includes the transcript of the interviews Russell filmed for the BBC-TV arts program "Monitor" with Ballet teacher Dame Marie Rambert (1959) and playwright Shelagh Delaney (1960).

3. Periodicals

BATI, ANWER. "Rudi's Rudolph," *Punch*, October 12, 1977, pp. 56-60. A feature review of *Valentino* which presents an intelligent defense of Russell's employment of poetic license in his biographical films.

CARE, ROSS. "Russell's *Lisztomania*," *Film Quarterly*, 31 (Spring 1978), 55-61. An insightful analysis of the film, which attempts to establish the biographical and historical basis for the fantasy sequences in the movie.

COCKS, JAY. "*Tommy* Rocks In," *Time*, March 31, 1975, pp. 56-60. A review of *Tommy* which details some interesting reactions about working with Russell from cast members.

DAVIS, PETER G. "Ken Russell's Film Studies of Composers," *New York Times*, October 19, 1975, II, 1, 3. This hostile assessment of Russell's biographical films, centering on *Lisztomania*, is dealt with in the foregoing text of this book in the treatment of *Lisztomania*.

DEMPSEY, MICHAEL. "The World of Ken Russell," *Film Quarterly*, 25 (Spring 1972), 13-25. A ground-breaking essay on the thematic thread which binds together Russell's biographical films, up to *Savage Messiah*.

FARBER, STEPHEN. "Russellmania," *Film Comment*, 11 (November-December 1975), 39-46. An insightful essay on Russell's films up to *Lisztomania* centering on the continuity of Russell's personal style and vision.

GRUEN, JOHN. "Nureyev as Valentino," *New York Times*, October 2, 1977, II, 1, 23. An important interview with the star of *Valentino* that sheds light on Russell's creative methods.

HALL, WILLIAM. "What the Blazes Is Ken Russell up to Now?" *New York Times*, June 23, 1974, II, 13, 29. A key article on the creation of *Tommy*, Russell's most popular film to date, indicating that it is not marginal to Russell's work as a whole.

KAEL, PAULINE. "Ken Russell's *Valentino*," *New Yorker*, November 7, 1977, pp. 119-20. As anti-Russell as her earlier reviews of his films, the reviewer again raises the right questions about Russell's approach to the biographical film genre and hence cannot be disregarded.

KOHLER, ROBERT PHILIP. "Ken Russell's Biopics," *Film Comment*, 11 (May 1973), 42-45. An important essay which places *Savage Messiah* in the mainstream of Russell's biographical films.

O'BRIEN, GLENN. "Ken Russell in the Port of New York," *Interview*, November 1972, pp. 9-11. A rather rambling interview with Russell about cuts in his finished films, unrealized projects, etc., which in sum is not very enlightening.

OSBORNE, ALAN. "Aftermath for the Artist Seen on the BBC Program *Monitor*," *Connoisseur Yearbook, 1964*, pp. 62-66. This journal of the arts devoted an essay in its annual special issue to a follow-up essay on Russell's TV documentary about four British artists called "Pop Goes the Easel." The upshot of the article is that the program brought well-deserved attention to the four young artists.

PALMER, TONY. "Ken Russell: Britain's Stormy Film Maker," *Telegraph Sunday Magazine* (London), July 16, 1978, pp. 36-42. Palmer attests that, despite Russell's faults, his telefilms on Wordsworth and Coleridge confirm that "he just is the best English film director we have."

RUSSELL, KEN. "Ideas for Films," *Film: The Magazine of the Federation of Film Societies*, January-February 1959, pp. 13-15. Written when Russell was still an amateur filmmaker, this article describes the creative process of making experimental short films and gives some provocative hints about his later work.

———. "I'd Rather Be a Composer," *Image*, April 1974, pp. 6-11. An unusually sophisticated discussion with Russell of his interest in music, photography, ballet, and other artistic influences on his work.

———. "Welles's *Citizen Kane*," *Books and Bookmen*, April 1972, p. 6. In his brief review of Pauline Kael's book on *Citizen Kane* Russell discusses the related roles of screenwriter and film director on *Citizen Kane* in the context of his own past experience of movie making.

SCHICKEL, RICHARD. "Ken Russell's *Lisztomania*," *Time*, October 20, 1975, pp. 61-62. A feature review of *Lisztomania* which contains helpful interview material with Russell and star Roger Daltrey.

———. "Ken Russell's *Valentino*," *Time*, October 17, 1977, pp. 98-99. An important review of *Valentino* which examines Russell's satire of Hollywood in the film.

WILSON, DAVID. "Ken Russell's *Tommy*," *Sight and Sound*, 44 (Summer 1975), 192-93. A fundamentally positive critique of *Tommy* in one of Britain's most influential film journals.

4. Unpublished Material

RUSSELL, KEN. Handwritten letters signed to Gene Phillips, dated from London, 1970-79. Russell's correspondence over this period recounts anecdotes and reflections connected with the making of his films from *The Music Lovers* onward, as well as information about projects that were ultimately unrealized.

Filmography

1. Television Films
Although Ken Russell's television films are not available for rental, the major ones, which turn up from time to time on the Public Broadcasting System and which are often referred to by critics of his work, are listed below. Their individual running times are not available, but their average length is one hour.

ELGAR (BBC-TV, 1962)

THE DEBUSSY FILM (BBC-TV, 1965)
Cast: Oliver Reed (Debussy), Vladek Sheybal (Pierre Louys)

ISADORA DUNCAN: THE BIGGEST DANCER IN THE WORLD (BBC-TV, 1966)
Cast: Vivien Pickles (Isadora Duncan), Alexei Jawdokimov (Yersemin)

DANTE'S INFERNO: DANTE GABRIEL ROSSETTI (BBC-TV, 1967)
Cast: Oliver Reed (Rossetti), Judith Paris (Elizabeth Rossetti)

SONG OF SUMMER: DELIUS (BBC-TV, 1968)
Cast: Max Adrian (Frederick Delius), Christopher Gable (Eric Fenby)

THE DANCE OF THE SEVEN VEILS: A COMIC STRIP IN SEVEN EPISODES ON THE LIFE OF RICHARD STRAUSS (BBC-TV, 1970)
Cast: Christopher Gable (Richard Strauss), Ken Colley (Adolph Hitler)

CLOUDS OF GLORY (Granada-TV, 1978)

I: **WILLIAM AND DOROTHY**
Cast: David Warner (William Wordsworth), Felicity Kendal (Dorothy Wordsworth)
II: **THE RIME OF THE ANCIENT MARINER**
Cast: David Hemmings (Samuel Taylor Coleridge), Kika Markham (Sarah Coleridge)

2. Feature Films

FRENCH DRESSING (Associated British, 1963)
Producer: Kennth Harper
Associate Producer: Andrew Mitchell
Screenplay: Peter Myers, Ronald Cass, and Peter Brett
Cinematographer: Ken Higgins
Art Director: Jack Stephens
Costumes: Shirley Russell
Music: Georges Delerue
Sound: Norman Coggs, Len Shilton
Editor: Jack Slade
Cast: James Booth (Jim), Roy Kinnear (Henry), Marisa Mell (Françoise Fayol), Bryan Pringle (The Mayor)
Runing Time: 86 minutes, cut to 65 minutes for export
Premiere: May 20, 1964, London
16mm rental: None

BILLION DOLLAR BRAIN (United Artists, 1967).
Producer: Hary Saltzman
Executive Producer: André de Toth
Assistant Directors: Jack Causey, Jim Brennan
Screenplay: John McGrath, from Len Deighton's novel *Billion Dollar Brain* (1966)
Cinematographer: Billy Williams
Art Director: Bert Davey
Production Designer: Syd Cain
Costumes: Shirley Russell
Music: Richard Rodney Bennett
Editor: Alan Osbiston
Cast: Michael Caine (Harry Palmer), Karl Malden (Leo Newbegin), Françoise Dorleac (Anya), Oscar Homolka (Colonel Stok), Ed Begley (General Midwinter), Vladek Sheybal (Dr. Eiwort)
Running Time: 108 minutes
Premiere: November 17, 1967, London
16mm rental: United Artists

WOMEN IN LOVE (United Artists, 1969)
Producers: Larry Kramer, Martin Rosen

Associate Producer: Roy Baird
Assistant Director: Jonathan Benson
Screenplay: Larry Kramer, from D. H. Lawrence's novel *Women in
    Love* (1920)
Cinematographer: Billy Williams
Art Director: Ken Jones
Set Decorators: Luciana Arrighi, Harry Cordwell
Costumes: Shirley Russell
Music: Georges Delerue
Sound: Brian Simmons
Editor: Michael Bradsell
Cast: Alan Bates (Rupert Birkin), Oliver Reed (Gerald Crich), Glenda
    Jackson (Gudrun Brangwen), Jennie Linden (Ursula Brangwen),
    Eleanor Bron (Hermione Roddice), Alan Webb (Mr. Crich)
Running Time: 129 minutes
Premiere: November 14, 1969, London
16mm rental: United Artists

THE MUSIC LOVERS (United Artists, 1970)
Executive Producer: Roy Baird
Assistant Director: Jonathan Benson
Screenplay: Melvyn Bragg, from Catherine Drinker Bowen and Bar-
    bara von Meck's biography *Beloved Friend: The Story of
    Tchaikovsky and Nadejda von Meck* (1937)
Cinematographer: Douglas Slocombe
Art Director: Michael Knight
Production Designer: Natasha Kroll
Set Decorator: Ian Whittaker
Music: Peter Tchaikovsky, adapted by André Previn
Costumes: Shirley Russell
Sound: Derek Ball, Maurice Askew
Editor: Michael Bradsell
Cast: Richard Chamberlain (Peter Tchaikovsky), Glenda Jackson (An-
    tonina Milyukova), Max Adrian (Nicholas Rubenstein), Chris-
    topher Gable (Count Anton Chiluvsky), Izabella Telezynska
    (Madame von Meck), Kenneth Colley (Modeste Tchaikovsky)
Running Time: 122 minutes
Premiere: January 13, 1971, Los Angeles
16mm rental: United Artists

THE DEVILS (Warner Brothers, 1971)
Producers: Robert H. Solo, Ken Russell
Associate Producer: Roy Baird
Assistant Director: Ted Morley
Screenplay: Ken Russell, from John Whiting's play *The Devils* (1962)
    and Aldous Huxley's book *The Devils of Loudon* (1953)

Cinematographer: David Watkin
Production Designer: Derek Jarman
Art Director: Robert Cartwright
Costumes: Shirley Russell
Music: Peter Maxwell Davies
Editor: Michael Bradsell
Cast: Vanessa Redgrave (Sister Jeanne), Oliver Reed (Father Urbain
    Grandier), Dudley Sutton (Baron de Laubardemont), Max Adrian
    (Ibert), Gemma Jones (Madelyn de Brou), Christopher Logue
    (Richelieu), Graham Armitage (Louis XIII)
Running Time: 111 minutes
Premiere: July 16, 1971, New York
16mm rental: Warner Brothers

THE BOY FRIEND (Metro-Goldwyn-Mayer, EMI, 1971)
Producer: Ken Russell
Associate Producer: Harry Benn
Assistant Director: Graham Ford
Screenplay: Ken Russell, from Sandy Wilson's musical comedy *The
    Boy Friend* (1955)
Cinematographer: David Watkin
Production Designer: Tony Walton
Art Director: Simon Holland
Set Decorator: Ian Whittaker
Costumes: Shirley Russell
Music: Sandy Wilson, adapted by Peter Maxwell Davies, with added
    songs by Arthur Freed and Nacio Herb Brown
Sound: Brian Simmons, Maurice Askew
Editor: Michael Bradsell
Cast: Twiggy (Polly Browne), Christopher Gable (Tony), Max Adrian
    (Max Mandeville), Vladek Sheybal (DeThrill), Antonia Ellis
    (Maisie), Tommy Tune (Tommy), Glenda Jackson (Rita)
Running Time: 123 minutes
Premiere: December 16, 1971, New York
16mm rental: Films, Inc.

SAVAGE MESSIAH (Metro-Goldwyn-Mayer, EMI, 1972)
Producer: Ken Russell
Associate Producer: Harry Benn
Screenplay: Christopher Logue, from H. S. Ede's biography *Savage
    Messiah* (1931)
Cinematographer: Dick Bush
Production Designer: Derek Jarman
Art Director: George Lack
Set Decorator: Ian Whittaker

Costumes: Shirley Russell
Music: Michael Garret
Sound: Robin Gregory
Editor: Michael Bradsell
Cast: Dorothy Tutin (Sophie Brzeska), Scott Antony (Henri Gaudier),
    Helen Mirren ("Gosh" Smith-Boyle), John Justin (Lionel Shaw)
Running Time: 103 minutes
Premiere: September 15, 1972, London
16mm rental: Films, Inc.

MAHLER (Goodtimes Enterprises, 1974)
Producer: Roy Baird
Executive Producers: David Puttnam, Sandford Lieberson
Assistant Director: Michael Gowans
Screenplay: Ken Russell
Cinematographer: Dick Bush
Art Directors: Ian Whittaker, Roger Christian
Costumes: Shirley Russell
Music: Gustav Mahler, adapted by John Forsyth
Sound: Ian Bruce
Editor: Michael Bradsell
Cast: Robert Powell (Gustav Mahler), Georgina Hale (Alma Mahler),
    Antonia Ellis (Cosima Wagner), Richard Morant (Max)
Running Time: 115 minutes
Premiere: April 4, 1974, London
16mm rental: None

TOMMY (Columbia, 1975)
Producers: Robert Stigwood, Ken Russell
Executive Producers: Beryl Vertue, Christopher Stamp
Associate Producer: Harry Benn
Assistant Directors: Peter Cotton, Jonathan Benson
Screenplay: Ken Russell, from the rock opera *Tommy* by Peter
    Townshend and The Who (1969)
Cinematographer: Dick Bush
Art Director: John Clark
Set Decorators: Ian Whittaker, Paul Dufficey
Costumes: Shirley Russell
Music: Peter Townshend
Sound: Ian Bruce
Editor: Stuart Baird
Cast: Oliver Reed (Frank Hobbs), Ann-Margret (Nora Walker), Roger
    Daltrey (Tommy), Elton John (Pinball Wizard), Eric Clapton
    (Preacher), Jack Nicholson (Specialist), Robert Powell (Group-
    Captain Walker)

Running Time: 108 minutes
Premiere: March 19, 1975, New York
16mm rental: Swank

LISZTOMANIA (Goodtimes Enterprises, 1975)
Producers: Roy Baird, David Puttnam
Executive Producer: Sanford Lieberson
Assistant Directors: Jonathan Benson, Terry Needham
Screenplay: Ken Russell
Cinematographer: Peter Suschitzky
Art Director: Philip Harrison
Set Decorator: Ian Whittaker
Costumes: Shirley Russell
Music Franz Liszt, adapted by Rick Wakeman, John Forsyth
Sound: Ian Bruce
Editor: Stuart Baird
Cast: Roger Daltrey (Franz Liszt), Paul Nicholas (Richard Wagner),
    Veronica Quilligan (Cosima), Ringo Starr (The Pope), Oliver
    Reed (Servant), Rick Wakeman (Wagner's Superman)
Running Time: 105 minutes
Premiere: October 10, 1975, New York
16mm rental: Warner Brothers

VALENTINO (United Artists, 1977)
Producers: Robert Chartoff, Irwin Winkler
Associate Producer: Harry Benn
Assistant Director: Jonathan Benson
Screenplay: Ken Russell, Mardik Martin, from Brad Steiger and
    Chaw Mank's biography, *Valentino: An Intimate Exposé of the
    Sheik* and other sources
Cinematographer: Peter Suschitzky
Art Director: Philip Harrison
Set Decorator: Ian Whittaker
Costumes: Shirley Russell
Music: Ferde Grofé, adapted by Stanley Black
Sound: John Mitchell
Editor: Stuart Baird
Cast: Rudolf Nureyev (Rudolph Valentino), Leslie Caron (Alla
    Nazimova), Michelle Phillips (Natasha Rambova), Felicity Ken-
    dal (June Mathis), Huntz Hall (Jesse Lasky), Seymour Cassell
    (George Ullman)
Running Time: 127 minutes
Premiere: October 3, 1977, London
16mm rental: United Artists

Index

197